CAMBRIDGE STUD

M000234825

The Structure of Emotions

CAMBRIDGE STUDIES IN PHILOSOPHY

General editor SYDNEY SHOEMAKER

Advisory editors J. E. J. ALTHAM, SIMON BLACKBURN,
GILBERT HARMAN, MARTIN HOLLIS, FRANK JACKSON,
JONATHAN LEAR, JOHN PERRY, T. J. SMILEY, BARRY STROUD

The Structure of Emotions

INVESTIGATIONS IN COGNITIVE PHILOSOPHY

Robert M. Gordon

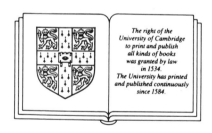

The right of the
University of Cambridge
to print and publish
all kinds of books
was granted by law
in 1534.
The University has printed
and published continuously
since 1584.

Cambridge University Press

Cambridge
New York   Port Chester   Melbourne   Sydney

Published by the Press Syndicate of the University of Cambridge
The Pitt Building, Trumpington Street, Cambridge CB2 1RP
40 West 20th Street, New York, NY 10011, USA
10 Stamford Road, Oakleigh, Melbourne 3166, Australia

First published 1987
First paperback edition 1990

Printed in the United States of America

Library of Congress Cataloging-in-Publication Data

Gordon, Robert M. (Robert Morris)
The structure of emotions.
(Cambridge studies in philosophy)
Bibliography: p.
Includes index.
1. Emotions. I. Title. II. Series.
B815.G67 1987   152.4   86–28397

British Library Cataloguing in Publication Data

Gordon, Robert M.
The structure of emotions: investigations
in cognitive philosophy – (Cambridge
studies in philosophy)
1. Emotions
I. Title
152.4   BP531

ISBN 0-521-33164-1 hardback
ISBN 0-521-39568-2 paperback

To Mae

Contents

Preface

Everyday talk about people is pervasively causal. Relations of cause and effect are implicit in nearly everything said about human action, communication, perception, and knowledge. The events and states we describe and attribute in such talk possess *causal depth*: Like sunburn and windburn, though less obviously, they come packaged with specific etiologies. The unpacking of these etiologies has been a major contribution of analytic philosophers of the past two decades.

Emotions might be thought insulated from such implicit causality because they tend to be identified with mere "feelings"; and feelings have traditionally been thought to be states that lack causal depth, states that are identifiable by their intrinsic qualities and without regard to their causes. This conception underlies the currently most influential psychological theory of emotions, that of Stanley Schachter. (As I argue in Chapter 5, it leads Schachter to misinterpret the results of some of his own experiments.) An increasing number of philosophers, however, find ordinary descriptions of emotional states to be rich in causal implications. Wilson (1972), Gordon (1974), and Davidson (1976) have made a special point of this, arguing that one is, for example, *embarrassed* only if one is in a state that has certain causal connections, particularly to beliefs and to "pro-attitudes" such as desires and wishes. Moreover, these are more than just the "typical" connections that, according to functionalist theories of mind, characterize *all* mental states.

A careful study of these implicit etiologies might enable one to answer a number of long-standing questions about the "emotions," or at least to answer them for a majority of the states lumped under that adventitious label. That was my hope and aspiration in setting out to write this book. Among the questions addressed are these: What distinguishes one so-called emotion from another – embarrassment, say, from anger, fear, or delight? Is it just that they *feel* different, as many philosophers and psychologists have supposed?

ix

What is it for an emotion to be *about* something? And what fixes its "content," the specification of what it is about? The etiologies implicit in attributions of emotions will be seen to resemble in some important respects those implicit in attributions of *intentional actions*. But we commonly suppose emotions to be *passions*, not actions. Hence people are not held responsible for their emotions in quite the same way as for their actions. Is there a difference in the etiologies of emotions and actions that might account for such intuitions?

A major obstacle to clarity and understanding is the term 'emotion' itself. The term is more vague and more vexingly ambiguous than most of the terms that designate the various states typically collected under that rubric – such as 'anger,' 'embarrassment,' 'fear,' and 'joy.' Moreover (as I explain in Chapter 2), the term 'emotion' retains the connotation of a certain false theory of what those diverse states have in common. Finally, it is not at all obvious that those states have *anything* interesting or important in common, anything that distinguishes them from all other mental states.

I was at first skeptical of finding any common thread among the various states usually called "emotions." Then I discovered that, with one's attention limited to certain linguistic forms of description – emotion verbs or adjectives followed by 'that' clauses or other sentential complements – a remarkable dichotomy becomes visible. The bulk of the so-called emotions fall on one side of the dichotomy: They comprise what I call the *factive* emotions. A few fall on the other side: These are the *epistemic* emotions. The members of each subclass share much with one another, and differ in many respects from members of the other subclass.

I decided to limit my investigation to these two interesting subclasses. This left a few of the so-called emotions out in the cold. A few terms typically said to designate emotions do not take sentential complements – 'love' and 'hate,' for example. A few others do take sentential complements but do not fall into either of the subclasses I was interested in studying – 'hope,' for example. Some putative twins prove to be quite unlike: *Being hopeful* is an epistemic emotion, whereas *hoping* is not; *terror* and *horror* fall on opposite sides of the dichotomy – the former being epistemic; the latter, factive.

The dichotomy between factive and epistemic emotions explains and replaces the traditional distinction between "forward-looking" and "backward-looking" emotions. Some have thought it a major obstacle to a causal analysis of emotions that forward-looking emotions are typically about future possibilities. (As some philosophers have put it, with less precision than they might: "How can the object of fear be its cause?") I find such states to be characterized not by *futurity* of content but by *uncertainty* (more specifically, uncertainty about matters not under one's control). This proves to be the key to a causal analysis of their content; it also helps us to understand why these states bear an important functional resemblance to *belief* (whence my term for them, "epistemic" emotions).

What I find particularly fascinating about the *factive* emotions is that their etiology includes an extremely strong epistemic condition: Standard ways of attributing them – without resort to circumlocution – impute not mere belief but knowledge (Gordon 1969, 1973, 1974; Unger 1975). This is of particular interest if knowledge itself is a kind of etiological package, involving causal ties between beliefs and the world. But the deeper significance of the knowledge condition emerges, I think, only when one examines the wider enterprise in which our commonsense theory of the emotions is embedded: commonsense explanation and prediction of behavior. In Chapter 7, as a postscript to this study of the emotions, I sketch an account of commonsense (or "folk") psychology, with an eye to explaining what I call the "normality of knowledge." The gist is that our attempts to explain and predict the behavior of others normally have an egocentric base: We explain and predict as if others shared our own perspective, *except* where specific adjustments are made, for example, for false beliefs. But egocentrism involves crediting others, in effect, with knowing anything *we* presume to know, that is, knowing whatever we ourselves count as "the facts." Hence explanation and prediction begin with a presumption of knowledge. This suggests, among other things, that a capacity to attribute *beliefs* (particularly, *false* beliefs) is not a prerequisite for attributing factive emotions. My suspicion (only adumbrated in this book) is that the concept of belief is a relatively late addition to folk psychology: that the attribution of emotions and the rational explanation of action were on the scene long before.

Acknowledgments

It was Irving Thalberg's article "Emotion and Thought" (1964) that first led me to see that there are buried riches in our discourse about emotions and stimulated me to investigate the topic. Although I disagreed with some of the conclusions of that article, my first inquiries were a follow-up on the leads it provided. Thus it is with special pleasure that I acknowledge also the helpful discussions I had with Thalberg in recent years.

Several others helped to shape, refine, and broaden my thinking on matters taken up in this book. The earliest work (ancestor to Chapters 2 and 3) owes a great deal to the influence and criticism of Fred Dretske and Peter Unger, particularly in my invocations of causality and knowledge. Donald Davidson's work influenced my thinking considerably, and he provided valuable comments and encouragement. On several occasions Robert Audi and Larry Davis offered acute but sympathetic commentary on much of the material in this book. Years ago, Arthur Danto helped steer me into analytic philosophy yet away from some of the irrelevancies of ordinary-language philosophy – a course to which I have tried to keep.

Other philosophers who provided valuable criticism of parts or predecessors of the book include Sydney Shoemaker – the general editor of the Cambridge Studies in Philosophy series – and John Barker, Wayne Davis, Bruce Freed, Harvey Green, Adam Morton, Paul Roth, Stephen Stich, and Raimo Tuomela. My critique of Schachter's theory in Chapter 5 benefited in its formative stages a decade ago from the comments of two psychologists, Howard Leventhal and Elaine Walster. I am grateful to Carl Johnson for introducing me to recent experimental work on the child's theory of mind.

Some of the material in this book was drafted while I held a fellowship from the American Council of Learned Societies in 1974–75. More recently, the opportunity and incentive to get on with it were provided by the University of Missouri–St. Louis in the form of a research leave and appointment as a fellow of the Center for Metropolitan Studies. Part of the revision was undertaken in the fall of 1985, while I enjoyed the hospitality and support of the Department of Philosophy at the University of Helsinki, under a grant from the Academy of Finland.

With pleasurable remembrance I locate the chapters of this book (or their predecessor articles): Madison, Wisconsin (2 and 3); Mount Hood National Forest, Oregon (5); Madrid and San Martin de Valdeiglesias, Spain (4 and 5); Kesgrave, Suffolk, England (4); St. Louis, Missouri (1, 3, 6, and 7).

Material from a number of articles of mine was incorporated into the book, in some cases with important emendations. For permission to use this material, I thank the editors and publishers of the respective journals: "Emotions and Knowledge," *Journal of Philosophy* 66 (July 3, 1969):408–13; "Judgmental Emotions," *Analysis* 34 (December 1973):40–48; "The Aboutness of Emotions," *American Philosophical Quarterly* 11 (January 1974):27–36; "Emotion Labeling and Cognition," *Journal for the Theory of Social Behavior* 8 (June 1978):125–35; "Fear," *The Philosophical Review* 89 (October 1980):560–78; "The Passivity of Emotions," *The Philosophical Review* 95 (July 1986); and "Folk Psychology as Simulation," *Mind and Language* 1 (Summer 1986):158–71.

1

Formal insight

On July 1, 2020, the centuries-old debate was settled by decree: *There are no emotions.* Thenceforward no one was, nor ever had been, in a state of "anger." The same fate befell fear, joy, embarrassment, amusement, grief, and all the rest: Banished from discourse, in private thought policed by (dare we say it?) guilt, they became unmentionable and unthinkable. For all the furrowing of brows, the narrowing of eyes, the clenching of fists (sometimes precursors to nastier actions), anger and its kin were, in the words of the decree, "Paleolithic fictions." The general terms 'emotion' and 'emotional' were, of course, outlawed as well – though these were hardly to be missed, save by a few philosophers and here and there an unenlightened psychologist.

Objectivity ruled.

HEBB'S EXPERIMENT

One hardly needs to speculate on the consequences of this fanciful ban. Something like it has already been tried, though in a less critical context: in the scientific description of chimpanzee behavior. A ban on talk of anger, fear, and joy in the higher ("anthropoid") apes may, of course, be better motivated than the one imagined above. Some of the publicity given to recent attempts to teach language to chimpanzees and gorillas suggests that many people, including even some scientific investigators, have a thirst for seeing humanlike attitudes and emotions, a perceptual bias verging on primitive animism. Why not, then, adopt at least experimentally the rule *Thou shalt not anthropomorphize the anthropoids?*

The psychologist D. O. Hebb reported the results of just such an experiment at the Yerkes Laboratories of Primate Biology (1946). His account, published more than forty years ago, remains

1

fascinating, and I find Hebb's discussion – his analysis of the human aptitude for "recognizing" emotions in the behavior of people and animals – philosophically more sophisticated than the bulk of philosophical writing on the emotions in the intervening decades.

Daily records were kept of the behavior of a number of chimpanzees, with the aim of pointing up significant behavioral differences between one individual and another – differences that might guide new staff members in their dealings with the animals. Over a period of two years, however, the records were to be kept devoid of all attempts to "anthropomorphize." Observers were enjoined to describe the behavior of the apes without recourse to the mentalistic vocabulary of what is sometimes called "commonsense psychology" (or, typically for its less favorable connotation, "folk psychology"). One might report that the animal moved its limbs in certain ways, perhaps even that it "attacked" an attendant; but there was to be no mention of any alleged thoughts, beliefs, or desires. Most important, there were to be no attributions of emotions and emotional tendencies: The animal must not be said to have attacked out of "anger" or "hostility."

According to Hebb, the records kept over those two years were far less helpful as a guide to new staff members than records drawn from the earlier "anthropomorphizing" years. It was impossible to learn which apes may safely be approached, by whom, in what manner. "All that resulted was an almost endless series of specific acts in which no order or meaning could be found" (1946:88).

During the anthropomorphizing years, on the other hand, distinctions useful for the prediction of behavior could be readily made:

By the use of frankly anthropomorphic concepts of emotion and attitude one could quickly and easily describe the peculiarities of the individual animals, and with this information a newcomer to the staff could handle the animals as he could not safely otherwise. (1946:88)

One example Hebb cites concerns two chimpanzees, Bimba and Pati, who on many occasions behaved in ways that were "superficially" quite similar. Each made violent assaults on their keepers, behavior that observers were unable to distinguish by purely "behavioristic" description. Analysis of the "objective" records revealed no significant differences in the circumstances, frequency, manner, or severity of their attacks.

Nevertheless, those who had known the two animals over a long

2

period, particularly those who had observed their behavior at times when they were *not* attacking, were unanimous in attributing all of Bimba's attacks to *anger* and Pati's to a *general malice* or *hatred of man*. The basis for this distinction, Hebb surmised, was that at other times Bimba "is always responsive to man, and acts in a way which promotes contact and petting by the attendants," whereas Pati is at best unfriendly. Some observers had indeed *thought* they could perceive a difference in the nature of the attacks by the two animals, but this was apparently a "halo effect," an attribution wholly due to the differences they had seen at *other* times:

Bimba's attacks seemed to occur only after some movement by the attendant that might appear like a threat, or like teasing; and it seemed that her attacks were always open, with the frank violence of anger, while Pati's were stealthy. But this was a fallacy of memory. (1946:92)

Although Hebb did not spell out the practical consequences of this distinction between Bimba's and Pati's attacks, one can imagine what some of these might have been. A prudent attendant, bearing in mind that Bimba, though friendly to man, is easily provoked to anger, would try to avoid slighting her or giving her insufficient attention – two of the provocations the attendants had mentioned. Pati, on the other hand, one had best avoid altogether, unless equipped with protective padding and a plan for escape. For it is in the nature of anger that it arises from – is "provoked by" – certain specific types of situations (or "cognitions"), such as a "slight," whereas hatred is a long-term disposition that, once established, needs no provocation at all.[1] (Still other "problem" chimpanzees – those that were shy, or afraid of strangers – would be best approached in a way that permits gradual "desensitization.")

Hebb shows quite effectively that superficially similar behavior sequences may be symptomatic of different underlying states, and consequently may presage different behavioral possibilities for the future. His experiment suggests that anthropomorphic description, _ *Cond.*

---

1 See Aristotle's definition of anger: "an impulse, accompanied by pain, to a conspicuous revenge for a conspicuous slight directed without justification towards what concerns oneself or towards what concerns one's friends (felt toward some particular individual, not man in general)" (1924: Book II, chap. 2). But "Whereas anger is always concerned with individuals, hatred may be directed against classes, e.g., any thief, any informer. Anger may be cured by time, hatred cannot. The angry man wants his victims to feel, the hater does not mind whether they feel or not; anger is accompanied by pain, hatred is not" (1924: Book II, chap. 4).

3

particularly the attribution of emotions and character traits, can be useful in allowing us to see, or at least to surmise, the divergent states that may lie "beneath" outwardly similar behavior.

Of course, one would be ill-advised to enter an ape cage confident that everything one believes about human emotions carries over to chimpanzees. Quickly one would learn to respect the toothy grin of an angry chimpanzee as betokening something other than amusement. No doubt, too, some scientific purposes would be better served by behavioral descriptions that avoided any implication of humanlike motives, emotions, or character traits. Yet Hebb concluded after his two year experiment that such "objective" descriptions had

... missed something in the behavior of the chimpanzee that the ill-defined categories of emotion and the like did not – some order or relationship between isolated acts that is essential to the comprehension of behavior. (1946:88)

Our traditional taxonomy of emotions, he writes, "evidently implies an elaborate theory," and its practical value in predicting behavior suggests that there is "some truth in it," as regards chimpanzees as well as human beings (1946:97–98). "Whatever the anthropomorphic terminology may seem to imply about conscious states in the chimpanzee, it provides *an intelligible and practical guide to behavior*" (1946:88).

BEYOND BELIEFS AND DESIRES

Hebb was not alone in thinking that commmonsense psychology is a valuable guide to behavior – suitable not only in everyday experience but also, with refinements, in the scientific study of behavior. At least in the study of *human* behavior, some of the concepts of commonsense psychology, along with part of its theoretical structure, appear to have been widely adopted by the behavioral sciences. Alvin Goldman has argued persuasively that

... much of the work done in the behavioral sciences either presupposes concepts quite similar to those of wanting and believing or frames hypotheses which are compatible with the operation of wants and beliefs. (1970:131)

Among the scientific or technical terms Goldman cites as typically meaning something like 'want' or 'desire' are 'motive,' 'need,'

4

'goal,' 'attraction,' and 'utility.' Terms that mean roughly the same as 'belief' are 'cognition,' 'expectancy,' and 'subjective probability.' (Goldman adds the weaker disjunct, "frames hypotheses which are compatible," chiefly to accommodate behaviorists, such as B. F. Skinner, who profess to give explanations that are *in*compatible with belief-and-want explanations. Goldman argues against such incompatibility.)

The so-called emotions have obviously not fared as well as beliefs and desires (or wants). Commonsense terms such as 'fear,' 'anger,' 'delight,' 'pride,' and 'embarrassment,' do not have their scientific counterparts, not at least in wide use; and the "elaborate theory" Hebb finds in our traditional taxonomy of emotions is rarely represented in scientific theories of behavior. Of course, scientists who use *belief*-like concepts to explain behavior may be interested in commonsense *beliefs about* such putative states as fear, anger, delight, pride, and embarrassment. For such beliefs, even if they are thought to have no place in scientific theorizing, surely figure in commonsense theorizing about behavior (one's own as well as that of others); and such theorizing is, arguably, a particularly important *influence* on behavior (see Heider 1958).

In sum, behavioral scientists have generally tried to get by without adopting and invoking the concepts of the various emotions. If there is an elaborate commonsense theory of such states, few scientists have been willing to give it their professional endorsement. One reason, no doubt, is lack of agreement as to the content of that theory, and hence as to what they would be buying into. A second motive for withholding endorsement is parsimony: If one can make do with fewer mental states, then one ought to. Why introduce talk of anger, joy, embarrassment, and fear if any behavior explained by these states can be adequately explained as a product of beliefs and desires alone?

Is there any reason, then, to deny the explanatory adequacy of beliefs and desires alone: to think that an explanatory scheme that embraces beliefs and desires, or their technical counterparts, could not get by without incorporating the various emotions as well? I shall answer with a qualified "Yes." Two fictional examples will be discussed: one concerning an emotion typical of those discussed in Chapter 3 (the "factive" emotions), the other concerning two "epistemic" emotions discussed in Chapter 4.

5

The book burning. Jones, the department chairperson, is having an affair with Smith, one of the new assistant professors. Jones is an unmarried woman; Smith, a married man. She gives him her book manuscript for comment. Smith takes it home and leaves it on his desk. The two drive to a conference in another city. Smith's wife burns the book manuscript, one page at a time.

Why did she do that? What *desires* might figure in the explanation of her behavior? Trivially, this might be one:

(*Db*) a desire to burn Jones's manuscript.

One might, of course, add that she believed a particular object to be Jones's manuscript; that is why she burned that object. But this is not likely to put anyone's mind to rest. The wish to have Mrs. Smith's book burning "explained" would probably not be satisfied by a belief-and-desire explanation that failed to explain why she desired to burn Jones's manuscript.

Such an explanation would no doubt involve

(*Ba*) a belief that Jones and Mr. Smith had been having an affair.

But what is the connection between *Ba* and *Db*? Why would *Ba* make her want to burn Jones's manuscript? A relevant presumption would be that she believed the destruction of the manuscript to be a bad thing from the point of view of the chairperson (and/or the husband), a setback or at least a slight. We are likely to explain *Db* by such a belief together with

(*Ds*) a desire to do something that would be a setback or a slight to the chairperson (and/or the husband).

Thus we explain what Mrs. Smith did by *Db*, and we explain *Db* by *Ds*. But how do we explain *Ds*? What is the connection between *Ba* and *Ds*? One possibility is that she had a desire to deter the two from continuing the affair. She believed that a setback or a slight in response to the affair might lead them to expect even worse if the affair continued. This might explain her burning the manuscript, though perhaps not her doing so one page at a time.

But suppose we add a further complication. On the way back from the conference, Jones and Mr. Smith die in an automobile accident. After their funerals, the widow burns the manuscript. Here one can't explain *Ds* by a desire to deter the lovers from continuing the affair. We might explain it by attributing to Mrs.

6

Smith a desire *to get even*: perhaps, by "evening the scales," to restore an abstract retributive "justice," or perhaps to restore her "honor" and thereby her self-respect. Even a posthumous setback or slight might seem, to some minds, to set things right again.

But one may find her behavior plausible and even "understandable" without imputing such a principle of posthumous equilibration. She needn't have been acting on principle at all. *Ba* could lead to *Ds* by a quite different path. Presumably she also had

($D^\sim a$) a retrospective wish that her husband and the chairperson *had not* been having an affair.

But *Ba* and *D~a* jointly constitute what may loosely be called a "wish-frustration": a belief that something is the case together with a wish that it weren't. (This usage is explained in Chapter 2.) And human beings are so constructed, it appears, that wish-frustration *frequently has notable effects*. It may have observable physiological effects and effects on one's competence in various tasks; more important, it may cause one to have desires one would not otherwise have had, and thus to be motivated to act in ways one wouldn't otherwise have acted. A particularly noteworthy effect is that of motivating one to do something to harm the person or persons who caused the wish-frustration. Wish-frustration often has this effect independently of any "deontological" principles of justice, duty, or honor and any instrumental aims such as deterrence. This characteristic motivational pattern approximates what we call "anger" (albeit "minimal" anger, without the motivational and communicational complexities that often enter in). Thus one can explain *Ds* simply by supposing that the wife was still *angered* by the affair, perhaps even more so now that it seems to have been a factor in her husband's death.

To say that human beings are sometimes apt to be angered, embarrassed, or ashamed is to say little more than that among members of our species there are certain typical effects, particularly on motivation, apt to be produced by wish-frustration, with particular types of wish-frustration tending to cause particular types of effects. (Not all the so-called emotions are effects of wish-frustration, of course; but as it happens, the majority of those for which we have names are. These are among those discussed in Chapter 3, "Factive Emotions.") Unless these motivational effects are recognized, there will remain, as we have seen, serious gaps in our attempts to explain human behavior in terms of beliefs and desires or their scientific counterparts.

The two farmers. Suppose that two farmers each wish that it would rain, so that the crops will not be ruined by drought. Each believes as strongly as the other that his crops will not survive another week without water, and each cares as much as the other about the survival of his crops. Farmer *A* sets out pipes in preparation for irrigating the land in case it doesn't rain. Farmer *B*, however, takes no such measures.

Such differences in action would be readily explainable if we could suppose that *A* believed it would not rain whereas *B* believed it would. Given the attitudes we are supposing both farmers to have, *A acts as if* he believed it would not rain: His dispositions to behave are, at least in most important respects, just like those of a person who was fairly sure it would not rain. And *B acts as if* he believed it *would* rain. But let us suppose that both are uncertain whether it will rain or not: They have heard from a source they trust that there is, let us say, a fifty percent chance of rain within the week. So neither believes it *will* rain; neither believes it *will not*. Nor do they differ in any other relevant beliefs.

The story is not at all implausible. Yet if motivational differences could be accounted for only by differences in beliefs or desires, the story would be *impossible*. But there is at least one other way to explain the difference in their behavior. For one can suppose that whereas farmer *A* is *afraid it will not* rain, farmer *B* is *hopeful it will*. One who fears or is afraid it will not rain will tend to act and feel like a person who *believes* it will not rain (but wishes it would). Likewise, one who is hopeful it will rain will tend to act and feel like a person who *believes* it will rain (and wishes it to).[2] There is an important motivational (and thus functional) similarity among fearing, being hopeful, and believing. Once again, serious explanatory gaps remain in any belief-and-desire psychology that fails to recognize these motivational analogues of belief. (These emotions are discussed in Chapter 4, "Epistemic Emotions.")

It must be admitted that, as is always the case, there are alternative

2 I distinguish *being hopeful* from *hoping*. One may hope without being hopeful; and it is the *hopeful* person who tends to act as if with belief. The two farmers example is discussed at greater length in Chapter 2.

ways of bridging explanatory gaps in belief-and-desire psychology. One might impute to the two farmers differing attitudes to *risk*, for example: A is more conservative, whereas B is more tolerant of risk. Thus A needn't be afraid it won't rain; he is simply cautious. But suppose that we have observed the farmers' behavior at other times, and seen no evidence of such a difference – or even seen evidence that it was B who tended to act conservatively. (Unlike in the case of Bimba and Pati, whose behavior "at other times" indicated that their attacks were differently motivated, in this case the evidence "at other times" tends to *rule out* certain differences in motivation.)

One might still avoid the fearful-hopeful distinction, for example, by speculating that farmer A had undergone a sudden conversion to conservatism or that B had undergone a complementary change in character. Or perhaps A has always been the more conservative *with respect to the survival of his crops in times of drought*; it's just that his attitude toward risk of this special sort had never before come to the test, this being the first drought in his experience. But in seeking alternatives to "emotional" explanations we are now being forced to "fetch" very far, straining credibility. (For an account of what it is for an explanation to be "farfetched," see Chapter 7.)

If one is to explain or predict human behavior in terms of beliefs and desires, then one should be prepared to introduce emotions as well into the explanatory scheme. That is the point I have tried to illustrate with the examples of the book burning and the two farmers. Of course, one can, as we have seen, find multitudinous ways around explanatory gaps in belief-and-desire psychology, if one is willing to fetch far enough. And that allows much slack to parsimonious theoreticians who would prefer to extract from folk psychology only the bare minimum of theoretical commitments. If parsimony is deemed more important than credibility, then one can get by without the emotions. This may partially explain why so few behavioral scientists have felt pressure to introduce the emotions into their theories of the springs of human behavior.

PHILOSOPHICAL INSIGHT

Remarkably many of the major classical philosophers took it as a major challenge to their analytical skills to attempt definitions of the various emotions: perhaps most notably, Aristotle in the *Rhetoric*, Descartes in *The Passions of the Soul*, Hobbes in the *Leviathan*, Spinoza in his *Ethics*, and Hume in *A Treatise on Human Nature*. What they were doing in their defining, I suggest, was to make explicit the elaborate commonsense theory that Hebb thought he saw in "our traditional taxonomy of emotions."

This is, of course, a theory that is far more widely *used* than *articulated*. When these philosophers come close to success in articulating it, they touch a nerve: Their definitions strike readers as apt, insightful, and revelatory. Consider, for example, a few of Spinoza's definitions (1883):

Regret is the desire or appetite to possess something, kept alive by the remembrance of the said thing, and at the same time constrained by the remembrance of other things which exclude the existence of it.

Consternation is attributed to one whose desire of avoiding evil is checked by amazement at the evil which he fears.

Fear is an inconstant pain arising from the idea of something past or future, whereof we to a certain extent doubt the issue.

These definitions impress us, I suggest, not because they nicely capture the nuances of ordinary expression – for they do not – but because they seem to tell us something about ourselves. Spinoza is explicit on this point:

I am aware that these terms are employed in senses somewhat different from those usually assigned. But my purpose is to explain, not the meaning of words, but the nature of things. (1883:178)

The classical definitions may be seen as answers to questions of the traditional Socratic form: 'What is regret?' 'What is consternation?' and so forth. Taken in the abstract, such questions might be thought to concern the meanings of certain words. But philosophers rarely pose Socratic questions in the abstract. Socrates himself, it is clear, had hoped that his own techniques for answering such questions as 'What is justice?' and 'What is piety?' would provide guidance, not merely in the use of certain "buzz words" but in practical matters of the greatest importance. Thus he asked, "What is it to live a *just* life?" for example, on the understanding that, once we have discovered the correct answer, no rational doubts would remain as to *how to live* one's life.[3]

3 Socrates is called upon to defend this assumption in Book I of Plato's *Republic*.

So, too, in asking what regret or fear is, the philosophers did not pose their questions in the abstract. Rather, they took it for granted that, whatever the answers to these questions may be, *human beings are in fact susceptible* to fears, regrets, and the like. Given this assumption, to discover what fearing and regretting are is to discover something about the susceptibilities of human beings. It is also, *perhaps*, to discover something about chimpanzees and walruses and groundhogs, given the more questionable assumption that they too are susceptible to fears and regret; and even, perhaps, about nonmammalian species and emotional robots of the future. But if any beings are susceptible, surely we human beings are. Given the mere assumption, then, that some beings are subject to fear and regret, to discover what fear and regret are is to discover something about ourselves. (The claims I am making for philosophical analysis are certainly not novel. Those readers who need no convincing might wish to skip to the end of this section. For others I offer a further illustration, taken from a different area of philosophy.)

An example drawn from the heyday of "linguistic philosophy" shows quite plainly how a philosophical answer to a 'What is?' question can at least seem to be telling us something about ourselves. In a classic paper on "Meaning" (1957), H. P. Grice tried to explain (among other things) what it is for a speaker to "mean" something by an utterance. According to Grice, one means something by an utterance if and only if one intends it to have a certain effect on an audience and further intends that the effect be achieved in a certain way. More specifically, what is intended is that the effect occur as a result of the audience's *recognizing* the speaker's intention to achieve that effect.[4]

Expressed in somewhat different language, Grice's "analysis" can be seen as a hypothesis that certain <u>*inferential processes*</u> go on in the planning of speech behavior. Roughly translated, the thesis is that when we have meant something by a particular utterance U, the utterance was "selected" on the basis of two complex predictions:

4 Subsequent commentaries have shown that Grice's analysis must be modified in some important ways. There are more radical problems with Grice's further effort to show that a similar analysis could explain what it is for words or sentences to mean something (as opposed to a particular speaker meaning something by a word or sentence).

11

- That the utterance of U would cause the audience to infer that U was selected because of the speaker's prediction that the utterance of U would have a certain effect e on the audience
- That the utterance of U would indeed have effect e on the audience, precisely *because of* the audience's inferring that U was selected because of the speaker's prediction that the utterance of U would have a certain effect e on the audience

It is unlikely that many people, at least before having read Grice's arguments, would have a ready answer if asked whether their meaningful utterances were "selected" in this way. They could say with far greater assurance whether they had *meant* something by their utterance, and indeed just what they had meant. Thus the definiens in Grice's analysis is initially more problematic in its application than the expression it defines. The analysis, if we assume it to be correct, would tell us that on those more readily identifiable occasions on which the definiendum applies – for example, where someone means something by an utterance – the definiens also applies. Now, when we recognize that someone meant something by an utterance, we can be equally sure that the utterance resulted from inferential processes of the sort Grice describes. We can also be sure that corresponding inferential processes go on when one *understands* a speaker to mean something by a particular utterance.

Spinoza's definitions seem to offer insights into human nature, I suggest, in part because, like Grice's, they tell us *what is going on* on certain more or less readily identifiable occasions: when we experience or undergo what we call "regret," or "consternation," or "fear." The definiens in any of Spinoza's definitions of the various emotions is initially more problematic in its application than the expression it defines. For example: On the one hand, we have been trained to *express regret* for things that have happened, and – by inferential procedures whose nature is not well understood – to *ascribe regrets* to others. On the other hand, we have *not* been trained to say when a "desire to possess something" is being constrained, in the fashion Spinoza describes, by incompatible memories. Spinoza's definition, if we assume it to be correct, would tell us that on those more readily identifiable occasions on which the definiendum applies – that is, when someone regrets something – the definiens also applies. Think of Spinoza's definition of regret as an invitation to reexamine those occasions on which a person, oneself or another, has (as we assume) regretted something. The definition

12

is in part a hypothesis that on those occasions something like the following was going on:

- The "activation" of a memory of a goal that was once attainable – a memory of it *as attainable* – was sustaining (keeping alive) a desire to attain that goal. (For example, going for a sail on one's boat, or seeing one's spouse in the evening.)
- This in turn uncovered other memories, reminders that the goal is no longer attainable. (One has sold the boat, or it was stolen; one is divorced or widowed.)
- These memories led to the *recognition* that the goal is no longer attainable.
- This recognition was (as Spinoza adds) felt as a kind of "pain" (i.e., "feeling bad").

Of particular interest is the fact that Spinoza's definition portrays regret as a state possessing what one might call "causal depth"; that is, an instance of it occurs only when a state (or event) of one type S_1 *causes* a state (event) of another type S_2. The activation of a memory "keeps alive" – is a sustaining cause of – a certain desire; other memories cause us to recognize the unattainability of that desire; and that recognition causes pain. The hypothesis that this process goes on evokes a confirmatory "Aha!" in many readers, seemingly enabling them to "see," in their own episodes of regret and in those of others, a *dynamics* that had not been apparent before. Further, to say that human beings are susceptible to having regrets is (on Spinoza's definition) to say something fairly specific about "human nature." It is to say that in human beings certain states are *apt* to cause certain other states, for example, that the "activation" of a memory of a past goal *as attainable* is apt to reawaken a desire to attain that goal, and that given such a reawakening, a reminder that the goal is no longer attainable is apt to cause one to feel bad.

UNIVERSALITY AND FORMALITY

Whatever "insights" Spinoza's definitions give us into the etiology of particular emotions, they are strictly *universal* insights. To apply the insights to a particular individual A, we needn't know anything about A beyond the fact that A regrets something, or fears something, or whatever. We needn't know whether A is a man or a woman, an Earthling or an Andromedan, or even, perhaps, a distinctly nonhuman animal or robot to which we deem it fitting to ascribe regrets or fears.

13

It is further true that these definitional insights are, as I shall explain, _formal in character._ Notice, for example, the repeated reference to one and the same "thing" in Spinoza's definition of regret:

Regret is the desire or appetite to possess _something,_ kept alive by the remembrance of _the said thing,_ and at the same time constrained by the remembrance of other things which exclude the existence of _it_ [my ephasis].

What Spinoza is offering here is a form or template to be filled in for each instance of regret. This becomes clear if we replace the emphasized expressions '_something_,' '_the said thing_,' and '_it_' with a dummy variable 'x':

Regret is the desire or appetite to possess x, kept alive by the remembrance of x, and at the same time constrained by the remembrance of other things which exclude the existence of x.

Or in my reformulation:

A desire to attain a particular _goal g_ is being kept alive by the "activation" of a memory of _g as attainable,_ which in turn awakens memories of something ("other things") that makes g now _un_attainable. (For example: g = going for a sail on one's boat, or g = seeing one's spouse in the evening.)

It is these "other things" that one mentions in specifying _what_ one regrets – for example, that one has sold the boat, or that it was stolen; that one has gotten a divorce, or that one's spouse has died. Beginning with the "recognition" that Mary regrets they sold the boat, one may not know _why_ she regrets this, that is, just what the relevant goal g is – she might regret it, after all, not because she'd like to sail it but because she'd like to pass it on to her children – but one can safely assume this much: It is some goal or goals that are (in Mary's view) _unattainable because they sold the boat._ This, of course, can be generalized in a formal way: If one regrets y, one does so because one has recurrent memories of some goal or goals that are (in one's view) unattainable because of y. Such generalizations open the way to what I shall call "formal insights" into the causes and effects of the various emotions.

AN APPLICATION OF FORMAL INSIGHT

Formal insight is exploited extensively in the following dialogue. This is a record of an actual interview in which a person (whom I shall call the "client") talks about one of his fears. Despite the

14

seemingly insightful conclusions at the end, it is important to notice that the interviewer exploits no prior knowledge of the client and indeed makes inferences solely on the basis of the client's answers. (The interviewer's comments and questions are numbered for reference in comments on the interview.)

1. What are you afraid of?
   Subways.
2. You have a general fear of subways. What is it about subways that you are particularly afraid of?
   I'm afraid of being mugged.
3. Afraid that you will be mugged?
   Yes.
4. What makes you think you might be?
   It's happened to people I know.
5. So that accounts for your fear. It would be unfortunate if you were to be mugged – and you can't be sure it won't happen, because, as you say, it's happened to people you know. Let's analyze your situation a little further. Is there anything you can do to make it *unlikely* that you'll be mugged? I mean within reason, of course.
   Yes.
6. What can you do?
   Avoid subways.
7. So you're afraid, really, of what would happen *if you didn't* avoid subways. That gives you a desire or tendency to avoid them. Sorry to ask you to spell this out, but it would help if you told me – just what is it about being mugged that you fear the most?
   I might be killed.
8. But isn't there something you can do – within reason – so that even if you were mugged, at least you wouldn't be killed?
   Yes.
9. What can you do?
   Carry a gun.
10. I see. So your fear of being mugged gives you some motivation to carry a gun. That would make you feel less vulnerable, wouldn't it? It would reduce your fear, make you less afraid of being mugged. That way, you wouldn't have to avoid subways. . . . By the way, this is not a recommendation. I'm much too stupid to tell you what to do. I don't even know what subways are. Or what *you* are, for that matter. After all, I'm just a computer – whatever that is.

COMMENTS ON THE INTERVIEW

As we learn from the final self-reflection, the interviewer is a computer, or more accurately a computer program. It was written to

15

demonstrate and test the analysis of fear offered in Chapter 4.[5] The above is a printout of a typical "interview." The interviewer is indeed rather "stupid" – by design, as well as by the severe limitations of my ability to program an "artificially intelligent" interviewer. As already stated, the interviewer exploits no prior knowledge of the client: For all it knows, the client might be a woman, a man, even an android or an Andromedan – so long as androids and Andromedans say they have fears. Its inferences are based solely on certain formal features of the client's answers – such as the fact that the answer to (1) is a single word ending with a single 's' (and is therefore almost certainly a plural noun), and that the word after 'afraid of' ends with an 'ing' not preceded by 'th,' and so on (and is therefore almost certainly a gerund formed from a verb).

The program is constitutionally unable to offer anything more than what I have called "formal insight" – insights into "what is going on" in the client that ought to be appropriate *no matter how the client fills in the blanks*. Yet I am inclined to think that, so far as it goes, my program discusses fears more insightfully than most people do.

It will be useful to examine the program's responses in some detail.

The entire point of (2) and (3) is to channel the fear "content" into sentential (or propositional) form. That is, they maneuver the client into describing his fear in terms of a particular sentence – specifically, the sentence that completes the form 'I am afraid that _____.' I shall explain below why it is crucially important to have a description that associates it with a particular sentence.

The client's assertion that he is afraid of *subways* tells us little more than that the blank in the form 'I am afraid that _____' is to be filled in with a sentence that is, explicitly or implicitly, *about* subways. (In the example, the relevant sentence, 'I will be mugged,'

5 Ager (1984) comments on the program: "Many of the precise arguments of the modern analytic tradition can find alternative expression in the idiom of algorithms and flowcharts. [Gordon 1980] describes the relationship between the content of an emotion and certain belief types in abstract quasi-algorithmic terms. His program is driven by that structure, leaving content to be filled in interactively. The program then is a testbed of the plausibility of the thesis when applied to various content and, not incidentally, a mechanism for exploring possible counterexamples." The program, entitled EMOTIONS, is written in BASIC. It borrows a trick or two from Joseph Weizenbaum's ELIZA.

is *implicitly* about subways: Its sense is captured by 'I will be mugged in the subway' or 'I will be mugged if I go into a subway.')

The second fear description, 'I'm afraid of being mugged,' comes close to giving us what we want. Given a gerundive nominalization such as 'being mugged,' the program is equipped to transform it, in (3), into a 'that' clause – in this case, 'that you will be mugged.'[6] The program asks for confirmation, however, because some gerundives would require a more complicated 'that' clause. Were someone to report that he is afraid of *flying*, for example, it would be a serious mistake to infer that he is afraid *that he will fly*. For – as will become clear in Chapter 4 – fear concerns (roughly) only those contingent possibilities *not under one's control*. Unlike being mugged, whether one flies or not is ordinarily under one's control, a matter of deciding to board a plane, and so on. The correct "translation" of 'I'm afraid of flying' would generally be, then, 'I'm afraid that *if I were to fly, then something bad would happen*.' That is what the program would propose, once the client has rejected 'afraid that you will fly.' Then the client would be asked for specifics: *What might happen?*

In (4) the program performs a feat more exciting than a mere leap in grammatical form: It begins to exhibit what appears to be psychological insight. It responds with a complex question, one that presupposes that the client does think there is at least a chance, a possibility, that the fear will come true, or prove true. This seems a justified presupposition. If someone were to assert that he was afraid of being mugged and also to assert that he was absolutely certain he would *not* be mugged, we would be justified in concluding – unless we questioned his sincerity – that he was simply *mistaken* in the way he "labeled" one of his states: either mistaken about his fear or mistaken about his certainty. (This point, like others made here, is elaborated and defended in Chapter 4.)

In (5) the program seems to "know" that what the client says in answer to (4) not only explains why he thinks he might be mugged but also explains (in part) why he fears that this will happen. Moreover, the program seems to "know" that in the client's view it

---

6 Gerundive nominalizations are flagged by the *ing* at the end of the initial word – once we filter out *thing* words such as 'something' and capitalized words such as 'Ming jars' and 'Corning Ware.' As the program stands, however, a fear of *mourning doves* would generate the response "You are afraid that you will mourn doves?" Not bad, considering that English isn't the program's native language.

17

would be a bad thing to be mugged, that is, that the client wishes *not* to be mugged – even though he had said nothing at all about his attitudes or wishes. (This does not depend on our common knowledge that people generally wish not to be mugged. Try substituting a fear of being *hugged*, and the computer will respond in the corresponding way.)

In (7) the program actually *corrects* the client's description of his fear: The fear concerns what would happen *if he didn't* avoid subways. Again this has to do with the fact that fear concerns contingent possibilities not under one's control. In addition, the program offers a kind of prognosis, saying something about what this conditional fear motivates him to do.

Finally, in (10), the program displays some of the things it now "knows" about the client:

· That he (she, it) feels vulnerable, at least when he doesn't avoid subways
· That by carrying a gun he would feel less vulnerable (because it would lessen his perceived risk, so that even if what he fears will happen *does* happen, the worst probably won't come to pass)
· That by getting him to feel less vulnerable, his carrying a gun would also get him to feel less *afraid* of being mugged
· That his fear of being mugged motivates him to do something to lessen that fear – thus, to carry a gun

In one version the program goes on to construct a customized causal flow chart – a block diagram that shows the causal chains leading to the client's fear of being mugged: how the fear depends on his uncertainty, which depends in part on his belief that people he knows have been mugged; and how the strength of his fear depends in part on the strength of his attitude toward mugging, which depends in part on his belief that if he is mugged then he might *be killed* – and the strength of his attitude toward being killed. It is then shown how his fear in turn causes a particular desire – which if carried out successfully would *interrupt* one of the causal chains at a particular point, thereby reducing the fear. (For details, see Chapter 4.)

It is remarkable, I think, that the input for all of this consists in the answers to seven questions, only one of which (number 4) asks for the *cause or explanation* of anything. The program squeezes so much out of so little by its use of formal insight. Filling in the blank in 'I am afraid that _____,' the client is in effect simultaneously filling in the blanks in a number of other forms, including the following:

- There is a chance (or: It is possible) that _____. (Alternatively: I am not certain it is not the case that _____.)
- My fear that _____ is caused by (among other things) my believing it possible that _____.
- It would be unfortunate if (or: I wish it to be untrue that) _____.

Because these blanks are to be filled in with a complete sentence the fear description needs to have a sentential form – or at least be susceptible to regimentation into such form by grammatical maneuvers. That is why the program maneuvered the client into specifying the "content" of his fear in sentential (or propositional) form, using the sentence form 'I am afraid that _____.'

Some of these forms have at least two types of blanks, two distinct "sentence variables." For example: 'The worst that could happen if _(a)_ would be that _(b)_.'

To fill in the second type of blank, here indicated by the dummy variable (b), the program must ask for a new input from the client. That in turn gives us a need for still further inputs, for example, to fill in the following form: 'Even if _(a)_, it probably wouldn't be true that _(b)_ if I were to _(c)_.' That is essentially how the response to question (1) generates the additional questions and observations put forward by the computer.

Although I submit that, as far as it goes, my fear program discusses fear more insightfully than most people do, the difference, I believe, is merely that it *articulates* better what we all in some sense "know." For example, we are *not surprised* when a person to whom we have ascribed a fear of being mugged takes measures to insure that even if he were to be mugged, the worst wouldn't happen. We also have some sense of how to "manipulate" such a fear. To induce the fear, *make people uncertain* about their safety, if they are not already, and make them think that they have *no control* over the matter. Or make them think that being mugged is likely to have very bad consequences, if they don't believe that already. To alleviate such a fear, make people more certain that they will not be mugged, or that they have control over the matter; or alter their beliefs about the likely consequences, perhaps by getting them to take measures that they think will reduce the risk.

We exhibit a similar wisdom in our dealings with a person we believe disposed to regret a particular state of affairs. For example,

19

if we are considerate we tend to avoid reminding a person of what he is disposed to regret. And if despite our caution the memory is somehow revived, we are not surprised to find indications of frustrated desire and pain.

After reading another chapter or two, I think the reader will agree that similar programs can be written for almost any of the so-called emotions. Such programs would exhibit comparable formal insights into such states as regret, anger, pride, shame, embarrassment, object-directed or "reactive" depression, and hopefulness. For my purposes these programs would be useful chiefly as an object lesson for demonstrating the extent to which purely formal insight into the causes and effects of emotions is possible. In doing so such programs make explicit the "elaborate theory" that, as Hebb surmised, underlies our everyday attributions of emotions and our ability to predict behavior on the basis of those attributions.

2

Pivotal distinctions

The word 'emotion' once meant a kind of physical motion: "a moving, stirring, agitation, perturbation (in physical sense)," according to the *Oxford English Dictionary*, which cites the following example from Locke: "When exercise has left any Emotion in his Blood or Pulse." The term then came to be used as a metaphor to characterize certain mental states.

Like the term 'motion,' 'emotion' is now sometimes used as a mass noun, to designate something we may have (or feel) a lot of, or a little of, or none of, at a given time. It is also used as a *count noun*. Anger, for example, is one emotion; fear is a second; and joy is a third. It is in this sense that we speak collectively of "the emotions." As a count noun the term may also be used to designate a *content-specific* type: Thus, fear that the train will be late is one emotion, fear that there will be a third world war is another; anger about Mary's remark is one type, anger about the referee's decision is another. Finally, the term is used, again in a count sense, to refer to particular *instances*, for example, Tom's fear that the train will be late, Mary's anger about the referee's decision.

It is important to notice that our linguistic forebears used words like 'anger,' 'fear,' and 'joy' long before the generic label 'the emotions' (or 'an emotion') was introduced. That label imports an unfortunate connotation: that such states are marked by at least a degree of "emotion" or (as psychologists tend to say) "emotionality." Although anger, fear, and joy often, and perhaps typically, are characterized by emotionality or mental turbulence, they are not necessarily, or always, so. And other states usually counted among "the emotions" are rarely if ever turbulent: sadness and gratitude, for instance, and being pleased about something. It remains to be seen what they have in common with the more "emotional" emotions. (The term 'passions' has often been used to mark off approximately the same collection of states as 'emotions' does,

21

but it confers a different – and more appropriate – connotation, which I shall explain in Chapter 6.)

In view of this confusion, it might be best to avoid the term 'emotion' altogether in any psychological or philosophical theorizing, as some have proposed (see Duffy 1945). Alternatively, one might just try to keep track of what one is doing with the word. That will be my tack. Where I use the term at all I shall use it as a count noun exclusively. And I shall try to keep a *careful* count, specifying particular lists of states in my attempts to generalize. If I err, I want to err on the side of undergeneralization, making claims that the reader may be able to extend farther, to some states that are not on my lists. In any case, I shall not pretend to be talking about every state we are wont to call an emotion, nor indeed that my generalizations do not apply to some states one might balk at calling emotions. The term 'emotions' will serve only as a rough guide as to the initial scope of this investigation. The final scope may be defined as *those states of which my generalizations hold true.*[1]

THE ABOUTNESS OF EMOTIONS

A good place to begin the investigation is to note a feature that nearly all so-called emotions share with beliefs and desires: Instances of an emotion such as anger are understood to *have reference to the world.* Suppose someone tells us that Mary is very angry. Or *something* tells us: the eyes, the mouth, the content of her conversation, or the vocal inflections. Immediately we want to know: "Whom with?" and "What about?" The more fundamental question seems to be 'What about?' For if we knew what she was angry *about*, it would generally be right to assume that she is angry *with* the person or persons – or, more broadly, agent or agents – she believes *responsible* for whatever it is she is angry about.

Why is it so important to answer the question 'What is she angry about?' For one thing, it appears that no one is truly angry unless he or she is angry about something, however general that something may be. So, finding a plausible answer to this question gives us

1 In entitling this book *The Structure of Emotions*, therefore, I might be thought guilty of false advertising. My excuse is that a more accurate title might be deemed inelegant: "The Structure of Amazement, Amusement, Anger, Annoyance, Delight, Disappointment, Disgust, Embarrassment, Excitement, Fear, Fury, Gladness, Horror, Indignation, etc."

more confidence in our initial hypothesis, that Mary is angry. More important, we need an answer if we are to anticipate Mary's actions. Without at least an inkling of what she is angry about, we can anticipate only the general accompaniments of anger, or more particularly the demeanor that generally accompanies anger *in Mary*. We might expect tight-lipped smiles and staccato interactions with her peers; we might be unsurprised to see her lash out at the least resistant target, the receptionist, and seek solace from the sweet old elevator operator. But will she barge in on the meeting? resign from her job? break into the personnel files? divorce her husband? sue the physician for malpractice? send a vituperative letter to the mayor? With no idea what she is angry about, we can only wait and see what her anger will motivate her to do. Nor do we know what if anything should be done to "make amends," and who should do it. Much the same can be said for most of the other so-called emotions. Unless we have some idea what a person is afraid *of*, we gain little of predictive value in learning that a person "is afraid." Moreover, if our concern is to see to it that there are or are not recurrences of a certain type of emotion – in others or in ourselves – we had better establish what the emotion is about. If we don't know what someone is now angry about, there is little we can do to see to it that we do not provoke him to anger in the future. If we don't know what someone is afraid of, it is hard to know what to do to quell the fear or to avoid it in the future.

SENTENTIALITY

To specify what a person *believes*, one typically utters a sentence, usually prefaced by the word 'that': for example, '(that) *Dewey was elected*.' Typically one utters it as a part of another sentence: 'Smith believes (that) *Dewey was elected*.' Specifying what a person *wishes*, one generally utters a sentence, though usually one with a subjunctive verb form: '(that) *Dewey were elected*.' What a person is said to *want* or *desire* is often a *thing*, specified by a concrete noun: an individual thing, 'that bicycle'; or something of a designated kind, 'a bicycle.' But even in the case of wanting and desiring, such specifications seem to be interpreted according to conventions and mutual understandings that add at least the elements of a sentence: Thus, where private ownership of bicycles is the norm, 'wanting a bicycle' is ordinarily understood (unless some *short-term* need is contextually indicated) as wanting (oneself) to have, that is to *own*, a bicycle. Yet one who "wants some ice cream" would ordinarily be understood to want to have, that is, to *eat* (not own), some.

If we are to find any systematic relationships between emotions and "propositional attitudes" such as beliefs, wishes, and desires, we had best focus on sentential specifications of what the emotion is about. Recall that in the fear program the client, by specifying what he feared, caused the blanks in a number of other sentence forms to be filled in accordingly. For example:

I believe it is possible that _____.

It would be bad if _____.

Because each of these blanks could be properly filled in only by a complete sentence, it was important to maneuver the client into giving a sentential specification of what he feared. It was not enough for him to say that he was afraid of "subways." The easy way to elicit a sentence would have been to ask the client to complete the form: 'I am afraid that _____.' But an implicitly sentential phrase, such as '(my) being mugged,' sufficed (except for the ambiguity noted).

Progress in finding systematic relationships between emotions and propositional attitudes would seem to depend on giving *primary* consideration to emotion verbs or adjectives followed by "that" clauses ('that Dewey was elected'), 'about' with an object that is a nominalized sentence ('about Dewey's having been elected'), and the like. In that way we can ask, for example, whether *believing* that Dewey was elected is always involved (to leave matters initially vague) in *being sorry* that Dewey was elected, in *being worried* that Dewey was elected, or in *being unhappy* about Dewey's having been elected. We may then ask whether *non*sentential specifications of what a person is sorry, worried, or unhappy about are implicitly sentential – for instance, like nonsentential specifications of what a person *desires*, interpretable according to conventions that add the elements of a sentence – or whether, at least, whenever a nonsentential specification applies (e.g., it is true of Smith that he is 'unhappy about the election'), *some* sentential specification or other must also apply.

If initially we narrow our attention even further to emotion verbs and adjectives followed by 'that' clauses, we are rewarded immediately with some dramatic results. A quite remarkable dichotomy becomes visible. Once that dichotomy has become sufficiently clear

24

we can abandon the restriction to 'that' clauses and turn to other ways of introducing sentences to specify what an emotion is about. Finally, we can examine nonsentential specifications. These expansions of the scope of our inquiry will come in Chapters 3 and 4.

BACKWARD-LOOKING AND FORWARD-LOOKING EMOTIONS

Let me build from the ashes of a familiar but in the end unsatisfactory distinction. "Backward-looking" emotions are said to be directed toward things, persons, or states of affairs that exist presently or have existed in the past. "Forward-looking" emotions are said to be directed toward future possibilities. Most emotions are backward-looking; among the few forward-looking emotions are hope and fear. Some support for this distinction seems to come from the tense preferences of emotions with a sentential content, and more particularly where a word designating an emotion has a 'that' clause for its complement.

Notice that one of the following accounts of what a person "hopes" seems at first glance a good deal more credible than the other:

· John hopes America will be on the winning side in World War III.
· John hopes America was on the winning side in World War II.

What is said of John in the first sentence is probably true of many Americans. But it is unlikely that what is said of John in the second sentence is true of many Americans. The same holds if the word 'hopes' is replaced with 'is hopeful,' 'fears,' 'is worried,' or 'is terrified.' But when other emotion words are substituted, precisely the reverse holds: It would be strange to be told of someone who was *glad* or *unhappy* that America will be on the winning side in World War III.

Using tense as our criterion, however, no emotion would be exclusively forward-looking and no emotion would be exclusively backward-looking. We can readily imagine someone hoping or being afraid that a certain train arrived late (past tense), just as we can imagine someone being glad or unhappy that the train will arrive late (future tense). We are left with two questions. Why are some emotions generally forward-looking and others generally backward-looking? And why are the train examples among the exceptions to this general dichotomy?

25

It is possible that the passenger on a train, wishing to finish reading a novel before his trip is over, hopes that the train will arrive late; whereas at the same time the conductor, wishing to avoid congestion at the terminal, is *glad* that the train will arrive late. What is not possible, evidently, is that the same person at one and the same time both hopes that the train will arrive late and is glad that it will. There is an essential incompatibility: Some condition evidently *always* holds when someone is glad or unhappy that *p* and *never* holds when someone hopes or is afraid that *p* (or vice versa). What we shall discover is that if a person is glad or unhappy that *p* then he knows that *p*, whereas a person hopes or fears that *p* only if he *does not know* that *p*.

This tie to knowledge would also explain why it is hard to imagine people being glad or unhappy that America will be on the winning side in World War III but easy to imagine people glad or unhappy that the train will arrive late. For it is hard to imagine people *foreknowing* which nations, if any, will win the next world war (if any) but not difficult to imagine people knowing ahead of time that a certain train (given its distance from the destination and its maximum speed, etc.) will arrive late.[2] We can also understand the disparity in the past-tense examples. It would be unusual for someone to hope or fear that America was on the winning side of World War II, because it is unusual for anyone (an American adult, at least) not to know this. It would not be unusual for someone to hope or fear that a certain train arrived late, because it is not unusual for someone (even an interested party) not to know whether a train arrived late.

A person *emotes* that *p* only if he knows that *p*, where the dummy word 'emotes' is replaced by any of the words or expressions in Table 2.1. For any of these replacements, '*S* emotes that *P*' presupposes '*S* knows that *p*.' I shall later refer to the designated states as "factive" emotions.

On the other hand, a person emotes that *p* only if he does not know that *p*, for any of the replacements listed in Table 2.2. For reasons that will emerge later, I shall refer to these as "epistemic" emotions. Only a few "emotions that *p*" are knowledge precluders,

---

2 I am assuming that one can know this without having ruled out divine intervention or the possibility that such "information" was planted in one's brain by the Evil Neurosurgeon.

Table 2.1. *Factive emotions*

is amazed	is amused	is angry
is annoyed	is ashamed	is delighted
is disappointed	is disgusted	is embarrassed
is excited	is furious	is glad
is grateful	is indignant	is pleased
is horrified	is resentful	is sad
is proud	is thankful	is sorry
is surprised	regrets	is unhappy
is upset		
feels ashamed (etc.)		

Table 2.2. *Epistemic emotions*

is afraid	fears	is frightened
hopes	is hopeful	is terrified
is worried		

or epistemic emotions: This short list is nearly exhaustive. All the rest, of which the first list is a sample, are knowledge requirers, or factive.[3] Although not every state that could plausibly be called "an emotion" appears in these lists, it does seem that all 'that' clause emotions – all substitutions for 'emotes that p' that are plausibly called "emotions" on our ordinary understanding of that term – either require knowledge that p or are incompatible with knowledge that p: They are either factive or epistemic.

These points will all be duly amplified and supported with evidence and argument. But first it would be timely to introduce another intuitive distinction among the so-called emotions.

NEGATIVE AND POSITIVE EMOTIONS

With few exceptions, emotions are intuitively characterizable as "negative" emotions, such as fear, embarrassment, and anger, or as "positive" emotions, such as pride and gladness. Thus, most of the states listed in Table 2.1 can readily be sorted into two lists, as

---

3 The important contrast that emerges when words such as 'embarrassed' and words such as 'afraid' are followed by a 'that' clause was first observed by Thalberg (1964). Thalberg was concerned with the belief implication alone, whereas I see the contrast as pivoting on certainty, factuality, and knowledge.

Table 2.3. *Positive and negative emotions*

Positive		
is delighted	is glad	is grateful
is pleased	is proud	

Negative		
is angry	is annoyed	is ashamed
is disappointed	is disgusted	is embarrassed
is furious	is horrified	is indignant
is resentful	is sad	is sorry
is unhappy	is upset	regrets

in Table 2.3, namely, those that designate positive states and those that designate negative states. (As the list suggests, there are remarkably few positive emotions – or, if you will, ordinary English makes remarkably few *distinctions* among the positive emotions.)

How can we explain this intuitive distinction between positive and negative emotions? In what sense are the former positive and the latter negative? One might be tempted to say that the typical *hedonic quality* of the former is positive, that of the latter negative: Typically, it is pleasant, or "feels good," to be pleased about or proud of something; it is unpleasant, or "feels bad," to be sad, angry, or embarrassed about something. One might also say that, because of their respective hedonic qualities, being pleased and being proud are *attractive* states, states we are typically disposed to being in. On the other hand, sadness and embarrassment are *aversive* or *repellent* states, states we are typically disposed *not* to be in. One must add "typically," however. There seems no reason to rule out the possibility that someone might find it pleasant, and therefore attractive, to be sad or angry, and *un*pleasant, and aversive, to be proud. It might be thought that these exceptions can be explained by distinguishing *orders* of hedonic qualities. There are ideologies, sometimes cultural and sometimes idiosyncratic, that make even ordinary pride repellent, and others that make anger or sadness attractive. Thus, although it always to some degree feels good to be proud of something, one may have a negative attitude toward such feeling good; and given this self-reflective attitude, feeling pleasantly proud makes one feel bad overall. By the same token, one might at times *enjoy* the unpleasantness of anger or sadness,

28

particularly if one has a certain attitude toward these emotions; but the enjoyment, it might be said, is owing in part to the *unpleasantness* of these emotions.

Although I think it is important to note these points, I do not think it satisfactory to let the basis for the negative-positive distinction rest in the pleasant-unpleasant or the attractive-aversive dimensions. One reason is that some qualifier, such as "typically," seems unavoidably to come creeping back in. That is, it may be *typical* that one who finds pride unpleasant overall or anger pleasant overall does so because of one's attitudes toward the first-order pleasantness of pride or unpleasantness of anger. But I can find no reason to think that this is *necessarily* so. A second reason is that it may be possible to make sense out of the notion of *unconscious* pride or anger, or at least of *being* proud or angry without *feeling* proud or angry. In such cases we could not call upon hedonic qualities to explain the positivity of pride and the negativity of anger. Finally, the first-order pleasantness (or attractiveness) of pride and unpleasantness (or aversiveness) of anger, whether universal or only typical, seems itself to call for explanation. Why does pride feel good? Isn't it because one feels good about something one believes to *be* good, or at least something toward which one has a *positive attitude*? Why does anger feel bad? Isn't it because one feels bad about something one believes to *be* bad, or at least something toward which one has a *negative attitude*? It makes sense that what one believes bad should feel bad – that is, if it feels any way, it should feel bad. That would seem to be part of the answer, at least.

In the end, the most plausible way to explain the intuitive division between negative and positive emotions is that they involve, respectively, a negative or a positive attitude toward something: in the case of factive emotions, something that is (or is believed to be) the case; in the case of the epistemic emotions, toward some epistemic possibility – something that might (for all one knows) be the case. For example, if Mary is embarrassed by (or about) the publicity about her wedding, she has a negative attitude toward there being publicity about it – roughly, a wishing there not be such publicity. But if she is *glad* that there is publicity, she has a *positive* attitude toward there being publicity about it. It is worth noting that the positive or negative attitude is not an attitude toward the emotion itself, for instance, the gladness or the embarrassment. Instead, it is an attitude toward what is loosely called the "object"

29

or "content" of the emotion. As I show in Chapter 6, this contrasts significantly with the attitudes involved in the rational explanation of action.

One might alternatively explain the distinction by saying that the positive emotions involve a positive *evaluation* of the object or content of the emotion, for example, the publicity about the wedding, whereas the negative emotions involve a negative *evaluation* of the object or content of the emotion. Thus, as stated, pride is about something one believes to be *good*, whereas anger is about something one believes to be *bad*. I have no problem with this provided that believing something to be good (bad) is understood to involve having the corresponding attitude – and nothing more. But it is at least arguable, on the one hand, that evaluative beliefs do not necessarily involve the corresponding attitudes: that one may believe something to be "conventionally" good (bad), that is, the sort of thing generally *said* to be good (bad) while being quite indifferent to it oneself: One wouldn't lift a finger to secure it, though one believes it "good"; one wouldn't try to avoid it even at minimal cost, though one believes it "bad." On the other hand, it is also arguable that unlike the concept of attitude, that of evaluation is closely tied to evaluative *utterance*: To attribute to someone an evaluation of something is to say something about what he would be disposed (sincerely) to say, if he were to say anything one way or the other. This affinity for utterance makes it more troubling, for example, to attribute evaluations (evaluative beliefs) to nonlinguistic animals, although one might be willing to talk about their attitudes, desires, or preferences. For these two reasons, I would prefer to speak of attitudes.

Some care is required in describing the relevant attitudes. 'Wanting something to be the case' and 'desiring something to be the case' describe attitudes. But these will not do as the attitudes generally requisite for the various emotions. One reason is that when S is delighted or angry about the fact that p, S already *knows* it to be the case that p. This leaves S with no possibility of *instrumental or aversive action*. In such a case the notions of wanting and desiring are usually thought inapplicable. Most obviously, where the object phrase is in the past tense the verb 'want' gives us a deviant utterance: 'I want the wedding not to have been publicized.'

For this and other reasons it is preferable to speak of "wishing" something to be so. Mary "wishes the wedding (not) to have been publicized." I prefer to use the accusative-and-infinitive construction after 'wish' in order to avoid the subjunctive mood, which in the past tense would presuppose that what is wished is contrary to fact. It will be convenient to introduce canonical formulas, as follows: When S is pleased (etc.) about the fact that p, then S *wishes it to be the case* that p; when S is angry (etc.) about the fact that p, S *wishes it not to be the case* that p.

It is worth mentioning another relevant feature of wishing. Not only is it possible to be ambivalent in what one wishes, that is, concurrently to wish it to be the case that p and to wish it not to be the case that p. More interesting, wishes are rationally blind to one another. That is, if I recognize that getting a certain wish of mine will exact an exorbitant cost in terms of other wishes of mine, this is no reason to give up or even to weaken that wish. For I may wish that getting that wish did not exact so high a cost; indeed, I may wish the world to be such that fulfillment of all my present wishes would be mutually compossible. (R. S. Peters [1961–2:127] quotes a colleague as wishing to be monogamously married to eight women at once.) This feature of wishing makes it possible for someone without irrationality to be angry at not having been appointed committee chairman, even though he strongly prefers not to have been appointed. It also makes it possible, again without irrationality, to have "mixed emotions" about something, that is, to suffer concurrently a negative emotion and a positive emotion about the same fact: to be angry about not having been appointed committee chairman and at the same time to be very glad, even delighted, that one was not appointed committee chairman.

When S is angry about the fact that p, S believes that p and wishes it not to be the case that p. Since what S believes is the contradictory or at least the contrary of what S wishes, we can say that S's wish is *frustrated*. (Since reference to 'the fact that p' presupposes that S's belief is true, the wish is frustrated in reality as well as "in thought"; but at this stage I am concerned only with frustration "in thought.") The same holds for all the negative emotions we have considered. The positive emotions, by the same token, seem to involve a wish that is *satisfied*. This point is amplified in Chapters 3 and 4.

It might be useful to put into a single table the negative-positive distinction together with the factive-epistemic distinction made in

Table 2.4. *The two distinctions*

	S wishes that not-*p*	*S* wishes that *p*
S uncertain whether *p* or not-*p*	fears is afraid is terrified is worried	is hopeful
S certain (and knows) that *p*	is angry is annoyed is ashamed is disappointed is disgusted is embarrassed is furious is horrified is indignant is resentful is sad is sorry is unhappy is upset regrets	is delighted is glad is grateful is pleased is proud

the previous section. In Table 2.4, I use '*S* emotes that *p*' as the general formula, the word 'emotes' to be replaced by any one of the verbs in the table. The presuppositions or entailments of '*S* emotes that *p*' are indicated for each of the two rows and two columns of the table.

THE EPISTEMIC EMOTIONS

If someone fears or is afraid or terrified that something is so, and there come to be strong reasons to *believe* that is is so, we say that his fears have been "confirmed." When there is conclusive reason for this belief we also say that his fears have been "borne out" or have "proven true." Under similar conditions someone's hopes or worries are said to have been confirmed or borne out. On the other hand, there are no conditions under which someone's *regrets* may be said to have been confirmed or borne out. Nor is someone's pleasure or anger either confirmed or borne out. In this respect, then, expressions of the 'fears' class differ from expressions of the 'regrets' class and resemble 'believes,' 'suspects,' and other *epistemic* or *cognitive* predicates.

These are more than niceties of idiomatic English. Recall the example of the two farmers discussed in Chapter 1. Two farmers each wish it to rain but are uncertain whether it will rain or not. But farmer A is *afraid it will not rain*, whereas farmer B is *hopeful it will*. One would not be surprised to find that A sets out pipes in preparation for irrigating the land, whereas B does not. Or, if irrigation and other measures are unavailable, one would not be surprised to find that A "feels bad" while B "feels good." It is as if A were already sampling the dissatisfaction that would come from knowing *for certain* it will not rain, while B is sampling the satisfaction that would come from knowing it *will* rain. Such differences in feeling and action would be explainable if A believed it would rain and B believed it would not; yet we have been assuming, rather, that neither farmer believes one way or the other. In short, it would not be surprising to find A acting and feeling like a person who *believes* it will not rain, and B feeling and acting like a person who believes it will. Thus the predicates we have been considering appear to have an explanatory function that in important respects parallels that of "core" epistemic predicates such as 'believes.' This functional resemblance might help to explain why fears, hopes, and worries are said to be "confirmed" or "borne out."

It would also explain a further way in which the epistemic emotions resemble belief and other epistemic states. Among the *reasons* we have for being afraid, terrified, or worried that *p* are some that very much resemble reasons for *believing* that *p*. I shall give an extended example. A superstitious man, John, enters the forest one evening, terrified that he will inadvertently step on a pine cone. His equally superstitious but dauntless companion, Jim, walks without heed. Not far into the forest, Jim waits for his cautious friend to catch up, when, lo! he discovers to his horror that his foot rests on an all too familiar object. He very much regrets that he has stepped on a pine cone.

Interested in their reasons, we listen for a response of this sort: 'Well, stepping on a pine cone is fourteen years' bad luck, don't you know?' or 'I believe that stepping on a pine cone brings down a witch's curse.' Our story would not be implausible if either man were to offer either of these as a reason, John for being terrified that he will step on a pine cone and Jim for regretting that he has stepped on a pine cone.

Such a response would be helpful in explaining why each man

feels as he does because it explains why it matters to each man whether he steps on a pine cone or not: It explains his strange attitude toward his stepping, or having stepped, on one. In particular, it gives John's reason for wishing not to step on a pine cone, and it gives Jim's reason for wishing not to have stepped on a pine cone. Thus it explains the essentially similar attitudinal components of their otherwise diverse emotions.

A distinctly different kind of response would be open to John, however. His response might be: 'I am terrified that I will step on a pine cone, because my eyesight is not very good'; or '. . . because there are lots of them lying around at this time of the year'; or '. . . because a friend of mine stepped on one last week.' Such a response would be especially appropriate if John thought it was not his attitude we wanted explained, but something else, namely, his belief that he would, or at least might, step on a pine cone. I shall say, therefore, that a response of this sort cites an *epistemic* reason as opposed to an *attitudinal* reason. Were John terrified of stepping on a rattlesnake instead, such a response would probably be the more appropriate one because we would probably regard his attitude as needing no explanation at all. At least, if his attitudinal reason were simply that rattlers, when surprised, tend to give a venomous bite that is bad for the health, he would have no need to mention it. But it would remain a reason of his, nonetheless; just as in the pine cone instance the fact of John's poor eyesight or the abundance of pine cones may well be reasons of his for being terrified that he will step on a pine cone, though mention of them would hardly diminish our curiosity.

Jim, it should be remarked, cannot have an epistemic reason for regretting that he has stepped on a pine cone. He has, of course, better reason for believing that he has stepped on one than merely the abundance of pine cones or the condition of his eyesight: He actually saw his foot resting on a pine cone. But if, when asked, 'Why do you regret having stepped on a pine cone?' he were to say, 'Because I could see my foot resting on one,' he would be giving a response, but not an answer. Nor can we attribute the oddity of his response wholly to the fact that it is his strange attitude, rather than his belief, that wants explanation. Had he stepped on a rattlesnake instead, such a response would again have been odd: 'I regret that I have stepped on a rattlesnake, because I could see my foot resting on one.'

34

In my story I spoke of John as being terrified, rather than merely fearing or being afraid that he would step on a pine cone, in order to ensure that my point did not depend on any of the variant uses to which 'fears' and 'is afraid' lend themselves. The verbs 'fears' and 'is afraid' may be used, in their first-person forms, to make a formally polite preface to an assertion, for example, as in 'I am afraid that my wife is not at home.' In addition, 'fears' and 'is afraid' are sometimes used, again usually in the first person and with a distinctive falling intonation, to suggest resignation to a fact, as in 'I'm afraid that we're lost.' In such uses it should come as no surprise that the speaker is apt to follow up his assertion by citing what appear to be reasons for believing. But my story could not have traded on such belief-implying uses, because 'is terrified' does not have such uses: One cannot, for example, suggest resignation to a fact with 'I'm terrified that we're lost.'

As the following pairs of sentences illustrate, if one is worried that something is so or hopeful that something is so, one may again have reasons of two kinds:

· Tom is worried that his wife was on the two o'clock flight, because that's the one that was hijacked (*attitudinal*).
· Tom is worried that his wife was on the two o'clock flight, because she said she'd be arriving early in the evening (*epistemic*).
· We are hopeful that someone will meet us at the station, because we haven't the money for a taxi (*attitudinal*).
· We are hopeful that someone will meet us at the station, because it is customary to do so in these parts (*epistemic*).

On the other hand, expressions of the 'regrets' class, followed by a 'that' clause, permit only attitudinal reasons. To show this I have assembled the following pairs of sentences. In the first sentence of each pair (labeled "1") we have an expression of the 'fears' class: Note that it comports quite comfortably with an epistemic reason. In the second sentence of each pair (labeled "2"), we have an expression of the 'regrets' class: Note that, by contrast, the expression in sentence 2 rejects an epistemic reason. Either we strain to read the 'because' clause as citing, implausibly, an attitudinal reason, or we find the sentence as a whole unintelligible.

1. He is worried that he missed the last train of the day, because the ticket window is closed.
2. He is upset that he missed the last train of the day, because the ticket window is closed.

1. We are hopeful that someone will meet us at the station, because it is customary to do so in these parts.
2. We are grateful that someone will meet us at the station, because it is customary to do so in these parts.
1. He is terrified that there are ghosts in the attic, because he heard a strange wailing sound last night.
2. He is horrified that there are ghosts in the attic, because he heard a strange wailing sound last night.

We can summarize by saying that a reason for fearing (etc.) that something is so is either an epistemic reason or an attitudinal reason. Something is an epistemic reason for fearing (etc.) that *p*, *only if* it is a reason for believing it at least possible that *p*. Something is an attitudinal reason for fearing (etc.) that *p*, *only if* it is a reason for wishing it not to be the case that *p*. Apart from 'fears' and its congeners, the only predicates that allow epistemic reasons are 'believes,' 'suspects,' and other "core" members of the constellation of predicates that designate cognitive or epistemic states, along with predicates that designate speech acts with which such states may be expressed, for instance, 'states,' 'maintains,' 'claims,' as well as 'says' and 'writes.'

THE FACTIVE EMOTIONS

I shall consider now the emotions listed in Table 2.1 – those I refer to as the *factive* emotions. First of all, it is reasonably clear that a person is amazed (etc.) that *p* only if he *knows or believes* that *p*. Of course, if my neighbors' quarreling produces a noise that upsets or annoys me, I am upset or annoyed *by* their quarreling, whether or not I know or believe that they are quarreling. In such a case, however, I am not upset by or about the *fact* that my neighbors are quarreling. Nor am I upset that they are quarreling.

More precisely, a person is amazed (etc.) that *p* only if he knows or has a *true* belief that *p*. There may be people today who fear or are worried that there are Martian spaceships circling the Earth. There may be some who confidently believe that there are. But it would be unnerving to hear: "Yes, and some people are quite *upset* that there are Martian spaceships circling the Earth." Or: "I have a crazy neighbor who is glad that there are Martian spaceships up there." For no one, crazy or not, is upset or glad that *p*, unless *p*. In the case of any of the factive emotions (listed in Table 2.1.), the truth of the 'that' clause is presupposed by assertions of the form

36

'S emotes that p.' (Or so it is in standard speech; but see below.) There is, as we may say, a "true content" requirement for emotions on the first list.

This is not, of course, to deny that there are people of whom we should say: "He is upset *because he believes* that there are Martian spaceships circling the Earth." That is typically the type of formula we revert to when we want to disavow any commitment on our part to the truth of p. We revert to specifying the "content" of the emotion in terms of the content of a belief on which the emotion is based. Try to tell someone of Smith's regret that Thomas Dewey was elected president, expressing yourself in a way that makes no commitment to the presupposition that Dewey was elected president. Does Smith regret having the belief that Dewey was elected? That says something very different. Perhaps 'Smith feels regret because he believes Dewey was elected president.' This may get the idea across. Strictly speaking, however, it leaves open the question 'What does Smith regret?' There is apparently no satisfactory way to fill in the blank in 'regrets that _____' or ' is upset that _____,' that does not presuppose the *truth* of the sentence (clause) used to fill it in.

It must also be added that in a novel or a psychiatric case study, where the context makes it clear that we are introducing the reader into the "notional world" of a person S, one may speak as if whatever S confidently believes to be true S *knew* to be true. In such contexts one might say, "He is upset that there are Martian spaceships circling the Earth," or even "He is upset because there are Martian spaceships circling the Earth."

We can begin to appreciate the significance of the standard presupposition of truth if we adopt a suggestion Donald Davidson made regarding indirect discourse. Davidson (1968) suggests that in an indirect quotation of the form 'S says that p,' we read the word 'that' as a *demonstrative*. Suppose someone has said, 'Smith said that Dewey was elected.' According to Davidson the significance of such an utterance would best be captured by placing the embedded sentence first, as follows: 'Dewey was elected. Smith said that.' The word 'that' is to be understood here as a demonstrative pronoun referring to the previous utterance or "speech act."[4]

---

4 Davidson quotes the *Oxford English Dictionary* for etymological support: "The use of *that* is generally held to have arisen out of the demonstrative pronoun pointing to the clause which it introduces."

Leaving matters thus, one would, of course, seem to be asserting, from one's own mouth, "Dewey was elected," and then saying that Smith "said the same." But in fact one may indirectly quote someone as having asserted something one regards as outrageous – or, at least, wouldn't be willing to assert oneself. One is not likely to be willing to assert, "Dewey was elected," for example. Hence, Davidson suggests that the "content" sentence (as we may call it) is understood as being uttered not as an assertion from one's own mouth but as a performance, as something uttered only "in the mode of play." The sentence frame 'Smith said that _____,' signals the hearer that the embedded sentence will be uttered in such a way.

Part of the significance of the "true content" requirement for emotions such as regret should now be clear. Unlike 'Smith said that _____,' the sentence frame 'Smith regrets (or: regretted) that _____' *does not* signal a play-utterance. There is no pretending here. One who says, "Smith regrets that Dewey was elected," *should* be understood to be asserting, from one's own mouth, two things: "Dewey was elected. Smith regrets that."

Typically, the content sentence would not be asserted *for the purpose of informing* the hearer of its truth. The hearer typically believes it already. The sole purpose of the utterance, as in the case of content sentences uttered in indirect discourse, is to provide a public "object" for the demonstrative 'that' to point to. But in the case of regret the object is not the utterance or speech act itself, nor a similar utterance by the person we are attributing the regret to. Although people do sometimes regret some of their utterances or speech acts, they also regret a lot of other things they do – and things that they may have had nothing to do with at all, such as a particular candidate's getting elected to office. An explicit reply to the query "What does Smith regret?" would likely introduce a sortal term, 'the fact,' as follows: "The fact that Dewey was elected."

Notice, however, that with the one exception of 'regrets,' the expressions in Table 2.1 are constituted of 'is' (or 'feels') followed by an adjective. Although these adjectives are among those that may be followed by a 'that' clause complement, they may *not* be followed by a demonstrative 'that.' Thus we cannot explain what is asserted in "Smith is delighted that Dewey was elected" by comparing it with the deviant utterance "Dewey was elected. Smith is delighted that." We may, however, shift the demonstrative 'that'

38

to the subject position, as follows: 'Dewey was elected. That delights Smith.' Or we may make 'that' an object of the preposition 'about': 'Dewey was elected. Smith is delighted about that.' For any of the 'is' + adjective expressions on the first list, either trick will work. And to the queries 'What delights Smith?' and 'What is Smith delighted about?' an explicit reply would be 'The fact that Dewey was elected.'

Some recent work in linguistics lends support to these maneuvers. According to a widely accepted thesis in transformational grammar (Kiparsky and Kiparsky 1970), the following sentences, despite "superficial" differences in syntax, are exactly alike at a "deeper" level of syntax:

· Smith regrets (is delighted) that Dewey was elected.
· Smith regrets (is delighted about) Dewey's having been elected.
· Smith regrets (is delighted about) the fact that Dewey was elected.

Of these three sentences the one that best reflects their common "deep structure" is the last; the others are derivable by various optional transformations, one of which deletes the explicit mention of a fact. In any case, these sentences appear to be almost universally interchangeable ways of specifying what a person regrets (is delighted about), and the last formulation provides us with a convenient name for the type of "thing" that is regretted. Even when we speak of regretting a particular *action*, this would seem only a way of saying that we regret *the fact* that we acted thus and so on some occasion, perhaps without specifying either the "thus and so" or the occasion. A person may be said to regret something abstract, such as "the rudeness with which he was treated": We may read this as 'the fact that he was treated (so) rudely.' Should he be said to regret "the way they treated him," we may understand this as 'the fact that they treated him the way they (in fact) did.' And so on.

Given what we may call the *factivity* of these emotions, when we specify what a person regrets or is delighted or upset about – without recourse to the 'because he believes' surrogate – we do so in terms of a "common world," speaking from what we presuppose to be a perspective we share with him. We refer to something that is as much a "fact" for us as it is to him. The significance of such factivity is, I believe, profound: It is that the concepts of these

39

emotions may be learned at a relatively early stage of cognitive development. Why this is so and what stage that is are among the questions addressed in Chapter 7.

The knowledge condition for factive emotions. The idea of a "common world" with a set of "common facts" about which people may have differing emotions involves more than an assumption that others share our *beliefs*. Two people may hold some belief in common, but the commonality may be pure coincidence. For example, Rupert believed, correctly, that Truman, not Dewey, was elected. But he had been ailing, and (as we say) "out of touch with the world." Rupert believed that Truman was elected, only because he was told so by a paternalistic friend – who, as it happens, had read headlines to the contrary but decided to protect him from "the truth." (The friend was being "untruthful," though what he said was the truth.) Unfortunately, the friend's benevolent deviousness *left* Rupert as insulated, as much out of touch with the world – with the political facts, at least – as he had been before, even though he happened to get the right idea about Truman. Although he was delighted by the news, his delight was not really about the fact that Truman was elected. Or so I shall argue (using a different example to make the point). To be delighted (about the fact) that *p*, one requires *knowledge* that *p*, rather than merely "knowledge or true belief." To show this will require that we pay fairly close attention to the way we speak and think when we attribute emotions to people.

Suppose we are among the few who know that indeed Martian spaceships have been sighted and identified. That doesn't help our crazy neighbor: We don't suddenly have license to say of him, "He is glad there are Martian spaceships circling the Earth." For, although he may believe what we believe, and thus believe correctly, he doesn't know what we know. When this is made explicit, we get what appears to be an inconsistency: "He doesn't know that there are Martian spaceships circling the Earth, but he is glad that there are."

There is, I think, a contradictory ring to each of the following sentences:

· He was glad there were Martian spaceships circling the Earth, though he didn't know they were.

40

· I am delighted that Truman was elected, though I don't know whether he was or not.

(In sounding these out, it may be advisable to stress the word 'know,' so as to bring out an implied contrast with 'merely believe.' Without that stress 'doesn't know' may suggest the absence even of belief – which would confuse the issue.)

Here is a different kind of argument in support of the knowledge requirement. This one makes use of a so-called Gettier example: roughly, an example of justified true belief that falls short of knowledge because the belief is held for the wrong reason.[5] Consider the following story:

Because John's new watch had been losing an hour every month, he returned it to the shop for repair. When he got it back, he reset it according to the radio. A month later he checked his watch against the radio and discovered that the watch was exactly an hour behind. What he didn't realize was that daylight saving time had just gone into effect. John was annoyed, of course, that his new watch was still losing an hour every month.

Note that whether it is knowledge or merely true belief that is required, the final sentence is strictly false – unless it is understood that the storyteller has switched to John's point of view.

Now suppose that not one mistake had been made, but two. Suppose the repairman had inadvertently switched John's watch with a similar watch belonging to a diplomat from Tanzania, and consequently returned to each man the other's watch. Then John, thinking the Tanzanian's watch to be his own, put it on his wrist and set it according to the radio, as above.

If it were merely true belief, not knowledge, that were required, then adding this second mistake to the story would make it consistent! For it is possible that John's watch, now gracing the wrist of a diplomat thousands of miles away, happens to be still losing an hour every month. Suppose it is. In that case, John's belief would, by sheer coincidence, be true. For John believes that his watch is losing an hour only because he believes that *the watch on his wrist* is losing an hour – whereas in fact *that watch*, which is not his, is keeping accurate time. He would have believed this no matter what his "real" watch was doing. He cannot be said to have *known*

---

5 Named after Edmund Gettier (see Gettier 1963). The story of the out-of-touch believer in Dewey's election is a Gettier-type example.

41

that his watch was losing an hour. But it is counterintuitive that the proper description of his emotion should depend on what is happening totally out of his ken, thousands of miles away. Anyone who assents to the claim made earlier, that sentences of the form '*S* is annoyed that *p*' presuppose the corresponding '*p*,' must, I think, agree to the further presupposition 'It isn't "out of *S*'s ken" whether or not *p*' – or, more strongly, '*S knows* whether or not *p*.' So '*S* is annoyed that *p*' presupposes both '*p*' and '*S* knows whether or not *p*.' In short, it presupposes '*S* knows that *p*.'

In the above example, John falls short of being annoyed that his watch is losing an hour, for precisely the same reasons, in the same ways, that he falls short of knowing that his watch is losing an hour. Similar Gettier examples can be marshaled in support of the claim that for any of the emotions in Table 2.1, '*S* emotes that *p*' presupposes '*S* knows that *p*.'

This presupposition helps explain why – despite the fact that they require *belief* that *p* – these emotions are not said to be "confirmed" or "borne out."[6] One cannot speak of knowledge as "confirmed" or "borne out" and do not take epistemic reasons. For we do not say that someone's *knowledge* is or has been "confirmed" or "borne out," because knowledge can never be said to be "false" or "mistaken," without contradiction; whereas only what is possibly false or mistaken can be said to be "confirmed" or "borne out." And, second, one does not have reasons, much less epistemic reasons, for knowing that something is so. (Certain things may qualify as reasons for knowing, e.g., the marital status of a job applicant – that is, for knowing what his or her status is, whether single, married, divorced, or widowed. But these would not be reasons for knowing, specifically, e.g., *that the applicant is widowed*.) Without calling on a full-fledged theory of what it is to know that something is so, we can give at least this superficial explanation. If there are reasons for knowing, for instance, that it is raining, then there must be reasons not merely for believing that it is raining but for having the true belief that it is raining. If there are reasons for this, however, it is possible to deliberate whether to have "the true belief that it is raining" or not. But this is not a possible topic of deliberation:

6 Unless this is glossed, "It is confirmed that he knows . . . ," as in "His knowledge of the enemy's location was confirmed by the tremor in his voice."

42

If one thinks it true that it is raining, one already believes that it is raining, and there is nothing left to deliberate about.

The knowledge condition for factive emotions helps support the view that the "content" of these states is determined by their causes, as I argue in Chapter 3. But it will not be until the final chapter that I explain what I think is the deeper significance of the knowledge condition. There it will be argued that knowledge may be attributed *by default*, for example, for want of the capacity to make allowances for another's ignorance. A very young child, or an early member or precursor of *Homo sapiens*, might be able to attribute knowledge, even though – indeed, precisely *because* – she *lacked the concept of belief.* Unable to consider alternate ways in which the world may be "seen," she credits everyone, in effect, with knowing what she knows.

SUMMARY

Guided by the traditional distinction between "backward-looking" and "forward-looking" emotions, we discovered that in the context of a 'that' clause complement, words that designate "emotions" (as we are inclined to say) fall into just two classes. For one class – those designating *factive* emotions – 'S emotes (e.g., is amazed, is angry, is delighted) that *p*' is true only if it is true that *p* and, further, that S knows that *p*.

For the other class – those designating *epistemic* emotions – 'S emotes (e.g., is afraid, is hopeful, is worried) that *p*' is true only if S is not certain that *p* (and therefore cannot be said to know that *p*). Indeed, S must also fail to be certain that it is *not* the case that *p*: in short, S is uncertain *whether or not* p. And S's *reasons* for emoting (being afraid, hopeful, or worried) that *p* may include *epistemic* reasons, which resemble reasons for *believing* that *p* (or for believing it at least epistemically *possible* that *p*). Finally, these emotions may intelligibly be said to be "confirmed," "borne out," or "proved true."

These considerations indicate a strong resemblance between, on the one hand, fearing (or even, being terrified), being hopeful, and being worried, and standard epistemic states such as believing or suspecting, on the other hand. We are led to expect *functional* similarities as well. And there appear to be such similarities. As suggested in Chapter 1, if farmer A is *afraid it will not rain*, one might expect *A* to act and feel like a person who *assumes* it will not rain – even though (as we shall see) *A* might actually think this *improbable*. Farmer *B* might actually think it *probable* that it will not rain, yet remain hopeful that it will; and *B*'s hopefulness would explain why B acts *as if he were confident* it will. When we discuss the epistemic emotions in detail (Chapter 4), we will come to understand better *why* they are functionally similar to belief.

Most words that plausibly designate "emotions" fall intuitively into either the "positive" class or the "negative" class. We found that, in the context of a 'that' clause complement, for the positive emotions, '*S* emotes (e.g., is delighted, is hopeful, is proud) that *p*' is true only if *S* has a favorable attitude toward its being the case that *p* – and, more specifically, as I argued, wishes it to be the case that *p*. For the negative emotions, '*S* emotes (e.g., is afraid, is angry, regrets) that *p*' is true only if *S* has an *un*favorable attitude toward its being the case that *p* – and, more specifically, wishes it *not* to be the case that *p*. Thus I claimed that wish-frustration and wish-satisfaction are involved in the negative and positive factive emotions, respectively. *How* they are involved will become clear, I hope, in Chapter 3.

Stated baldly and boldly, my view is that wish-frustration and wish-satisfaction each have certain characteristic *effects* on human beings. We use words such as 'upset,' 'sad,' and 'glad' to baptize some of these effects. Moreover, certain *types* of wish-frustration and wish-satisfaction – particularly those coming from a certain *source* – may have special types of effects; for example, a wish frustrated because of another's ill will (to put it roughly) is apt to produce a desire to harm that other person. We use words such as 'angry,' 'indignant,' 'embarrassed,' and 'proud' to name the special effects of particular types of wish-frustration or wish-satisfaction. It may be useful to keep this broad picture in sight as we plunge back into the thicket of detailed analysis.

3

Factive emotions

Some philosophers have thought it important, perhaps indeed the chief task of a philosophical treatment of the emotions, to analyze "the relation between an emotion and its object." One problem with such a project is that it is not clear what is meant by "the object" (sometimes, "intentional object") of an emotion. Metaphors such as "the target" of the emotion, or that toward which the emotion "is directed," offer at most a semblance of understanding. Furthermore, reference to "*the* relation between an emotion and its object" quickly proves to be a nonstarter. It lures one into such faulty reasoning as the following, which is a paraphrase of Kenny (1963:71–75 and passim): "There are many cases in which it is natural to think of the object of emotion as its *cause*: e.g., 'I was angry because he burst in without knocking,' and, 'Her behavior made me most embarrassed.' But there are other examples that show that the relation of an emotion to its object cannot be one of effect to cause: e.g., 'I dread the next war,' and, 'I hope Eclipse will win.' So, despite appearances, the ostensibly causal expressions ('because,' 'made me') must be understood as having a special noncausal sense."[1]

What is missing from Kenny's reasoning is some reason for thinking that, despite appearances, the same relation holds between, on the one hand, one's anger and the remark that makes one angry; and, on the other hand, one's dread and the possible future war that one dreads. Without such reason, the dreaded war poses no threat to a causal interpretation of 'I was angry because _____,' or '_____ made me embarrassed.'

I make no pretense of analyzing "the relation between an emotion

---

1 I believe I have given an accurate representation of Kenny's reasoning. My narrow focus on this fallacy should not be taken to belittle Kenny's book, a seminal work in the philosophy of action and emotion.

and its object." Thus far, indeed, I have focused my attention on sentences of the form '*S* emotes that *p*.' For my interest has been in the logical differences that emerge when terms we think of as designating "emotions" are followed by a 'that' clause complement. Without that narrow and relatively precise focus, I would not have been able to develop the distinction between factive and epistemic emotions. Had I tried instead to analyze "the relation between an emotion and its object," I might still be speaking of "backward-looking" and "forward-looking" emotions.

I can now broaden my focus considerably. For in this chapter I shall be examining the formal structure of the *factive* emotions. And where factive emotions are concerned, the following forms are, as I have argued, nearly always interchangeable – at least so far as the claims I shall make about formal structure are concerned:

· *S* emotes that *p*.
· *p*. S emotes (about) that.
· *S* emotes (about) the fact that *p*.
· *S* emotes (about) its being the case that *p*.[2]

The structural analysis I shall be offering can easily be seen to apply equally to any of the following formulations:

· He regrets (or: is angry) that she was treated rudely.
· She was treated rudely. He regrets (is angry about) that.
· He regrets (is angry about) the fact that she was treated rudely.
· He regrets (is angry about) her having been treated rudely.

Indeed, after a factive emotion-designating term, almost any form of noun phrase demands a sentential, and hence in this context a factlike, interpretation. For example: 'the rudeness with which she was treated' = 'the fact that she was treated (so) rudely'; 'the way she was treated' = 'the fact that she was treated the way she (in fact) was.' 'They regret the incident' = 'They regret (the fact) that the incident occurred.' It may be granted that concrete nouns – 'Jeremy is angry about *his lawn*,' and the like – typically do not convey enough information to yield a unique factive interpretation. Nonetheless, it appears that there is always a fact (or putative fact) in the offing, which the context of utterance usually enables one to pick out. Thus, if Jeremy is angry about his lawn, there is, as we might put it, *something about* his lawn that he is angry about,

---

2 A canonical stand-in for gerundive nominalizations in general.

such as the fact that it is bare, or simply the fact that it looks the way (in fact) it does.

BELIEF-DEPENDENCY

Suppose that Junior has monkeyed with Daddy's camera; he has opened the back, fogging the film and ruining twenty irreplaceable shots of Hong Kong. Daddy, as he comes home to this scene, happens already to be fuming over the fact that his car will be laid up at the repair shop for another day. He is angry. Now he learns about Junior's misdeed. He takes it to be a fact that Junior has ruined the Hong Kong shots. He *knows* that Junior has ruined the Hong Kong shots.

Initially it is a mere *coincidence* that he believes that Junior ruined the pictures and at the same time is *angry*. At some point it may cease to be a coincidence. It *must* cease to be a coincidence, I maintain, if we are to speak of him as angry about the fact that Junior has ruined the Hong Kong shots (or: about Junior's having ruined the Hong Kong shots). His anger must acquire a new "footing" in his belief that Junior has ruined the Hong Kong shots; or, to complement that metaphor with others, it must gain new sustenance from that source, and hence a new lease on life. The point of these metaphors is roughly this: Whereas formerly he would not have been angry were it not for the fact (or his belief) that his car would be laid up, this is no longer true; for the new belief – namely, that Junior has ruined the Hong Kong shots – is sufficient, under the circumstances, to make or to keep him angry. Thus it is no longer a mere coincidence that on the one hand he believes that Junior has ruined the shots and on the other hand he is angry.

Should it *remain* a mere coincidence, then he is not angry *about Junior's having ruined the pictures.* The fact that he happens to have been angry at the time he learned of Junior's misdeed is irrelevant: He is no closer to being angry about Junior's having ruined the pictures than if he had not been angry at all. His having the belief and his being angry must be *related* in such a way that it is not a mere coincidence that, on the one hand, he believes that Junior has ruined the shots and, on the other hand, he is angry.

Strictly speaking, his old belief (that his car would be laid up) may still be needed to sustain his anger. For one thing, it appears to be a datum of psychology that anger sometimes begets anger:

47

More precisely, in a sense to be explained in the following section, it is sometimes a *catalyst* for further anger. Thus, had Daddy not been raised to a sufficient pitch of anger by his belief (a) that his car would be laid up, it is possible that his belief (b) that Junior had ruined the Hong Kong shots would not have been sufficient, under the remaining circumstances, to make or to keep him angry. In such a case, he would not have been angry at all, had he not *also* believed (a). So what is crucial in the above example is not *that belief (a) is no longer necessary*, that is, that Daddy might have been angry, under the circumstances, even without that belief; but rather, simply, *that belief (b) is sufficient, under the circumstances, to make or to keep him angry*. We can show this more directly by supposing that through some bizarre connection, Daddy would not have *cared* about Junior's ruining the Hong Kong shots but for the fact that his car would be laid up. (A more perspicuous example of this sort is the following: Sam is angry about having to go to work at 6:00 A.M. and also angry about his neighbor's late-evening violin-playing. But he wouldn't have cared about the violin-playing, except that he had to go to work at 6:00 A.M. The belief that he had to go to work at 6:00 thus remains necessary in either case, violin-playing or no violin-playing.)

My position can now be generalized. There is a Belief Condition (BC) for being angry about a fact, as follows:

(BC) If S is angry about the fact that p, then S's believing that p is sufficient for S to be angry, given some existing conditions that are not themselves sufficient for S to be angry.

Note that BC stipulates only that there exist *some* conditions c such that c conjointly with S's belief suffice for S to be angry, where c alone do not suffice. There might exist *other* conditions, however, that do suffice for S to be angry, even apart from S's belief that p. As to the notion of "sufficiency," I understand it to have the force of the 'if-then' of subjunctive conditionals. Thus, not only is it true that whenever c obtains and S believes that p, then S is angry; further, whenever c obtains and S does not believe that p, the following subjunctive conditional will be true: 'If S were to believe that p, then S would be angry.'

Perhaps it is worth mentioning that I do not regard (BC) as committing me to determinism in any form. Should someone maintain that an element of *assent* is involved whenever a person becomes

48

angry, and that assent is an act, and that acts do not have causally sufficient conditions, I need not dispute with him here. Obviously such assent is not of itself *sufficient* for anger. If it is *necessary*, we must number it among the conditions c, that is, among the conditions that although alone they do not suffice for S's anger, do suffice in conjunction with S's belief that p. Even if such assent lacked causally sufficient conditions, this would not show that anger does not have causally sufficient conditions. This point is developed further in Chapter 6.

SOME A PRIORI LIMITS OF PSYCHOPHARMACOLOGY

The force of BC can be shown by the following example. With a sufficient dosage of the right drug, it would seem possible to put any subject into a state of depression or a state of elation. I shall assume for now that a state of being *angry* can be induced in the same way. (As we shall see in a later section of this chapter, BC makes such an assumption doubtful, if being angry requires being angry about something.)

Suppose that S, a subject in a psychological experiment, has been filling out a tiresome and intrusive questionnaire, and that while doing this S has grown angry. But suppose all that is causing S to be angry is a drug recently introduced into S's bloodstream by injection; and that, in particular, no belief of S's is a causal factor in S's being angry. S is aware that he is angry but is not aware that his being angry has anything to do with the drug in his bloodstream. (Either he is unaware that he was given an injection, or he was led to believe that the drug injected had a quite different effect.) S takes himself to be angry about the questionnaire he is required to fill out – more specifically, about the fact that he is required to fill out so tiresome and intrusive a questionnaire.[3]

The problem is to decide whether, under these circumstances, S is actually angry about the questionnaire, or indeed whether S is angry about anything at all. It would appear that BC requires that both questions be answered in the negative. But before applying

3 This "experiment" was suggested by the adrenaline experiment described in Schachter and Singer (1962). Their experiment is described and criticized at length in Chapter 5.

49

BC to this example, we need to sharpen the distinction between the drug described and other possible drugs.

The drug described is to be distinguished from a drug that although incapable of inducing anger on its own, increases the irritability of the subject so as to make him susceptible to anger at things that otherwise would not have made him angry – for example, things too trivial or too remote, such as minor slights and distant wars. A drug of this sort would have to work in complicity with the subject's beliefs, for by itself it does no more than lower the threshold of anger. I shall call such a drug an *anger catalyst*. (As we saw in the preceding section, anger itself may act as an anger catalyst, in this sense.) By contrast, a drug of the sort described – one that induces anger without the help of any belief – I shall call an *anger agent*.

For the sake of completeness, we should also distinguish between an anger agent and a belief-inducing drug, that is, a *belief agent*. For a belief agent may on occasion induce a belief that suffices, under the circumstances, to make a person angry. Like an anger agent (and unlike an anger catalyst) it does not work *in conjunction with* the subject's existing beliefs. But unlike an anger agent it does not induce anger directly; that is, it induces anger only by inducing a belief.

In our original experiment the subject was administered an anger agent. It was further stipulated that the drug (together, of course, with the required background conditions) was *all* that was causing S to be angry: This was meant to rule out causal overdetermination. Thus there was no belief of S's that also sufficed, under the circumstances, for S to be angry. According to BC, therefore, S was not angry about the questionnaire. S was not angry *about* anything at all.

Although my intuitions regarding the experiment match this result, it is difficult for me to estimate to what degree they have been shaped by a prior commitment to BC. In fairness, I should say that I have at times felt some inclination to ask, "Isn't what S is angry about just a matter of *how* S *feels*, and isn't this entirely separate from the question of what is causing S to feel this way?" To cut to what I think is the heart of the problem, what stands behind this objection is the principle that what a person sincerely reports himself angry about is the final arbiter of what he is presently angry about; or the related principle that what a person is angry

50

about is entirely a matter of how he feels, in a sense in which to feel a certain way and to seem (to oneself) to feel that way are indistinguishable states. After two preliminary skirmishes, I shall offer what I consider to be two telling objections to the first of these principles. Appropriately modified, they apply also to the second.

First, people misreport that they are angry about "the fact" that something is so, when in fact it is not so. Smith is *not* angry about "the fact that Dewey was elected" if it is not a fact that Dewey was elected, no matter what Smith may report.

Second, many people do not like to admit to themselves that they can get angry about certain things. A father unwilling to admit that he is angry about his daughter's intention to marry may prefer to see himself as being angry over her particular choice of a marriage partner. Assuming that he would have been angry no matter whom she had chosen, so long as she intended to marry someone, BC leads to what again seems the right conclusion, namely, that he is angry about her intending to marry rather than about her particular choice of partner. Whatever we think of psychoanalytic examples in general, it is hard to deny that one's beliefs as to what one is angry about may, like other beliefs, be responsive to one's wishes.

The following objections, I think, are decisive. First, if someone's sincere report can be shown to be based on ignorance, it loses any claim it might otherwise have had to being the final arbiter of its own truth.[4] Suppose that the subject in our experiment would not have taken himself to be angry about the questionnaire, had he known that it was the drug, and not any of his beliefs, that was causing him to be angry. It is thanks to his ignorance of the true cause of his anger that he reports himself to be angry about the questionnaire. This not only would undermine the report's claim to being the final arbiter but would spoil its value even as *evidence* of its own truth.

Finally, the first-person report is only one of many ways in which one's anger may make itself manifest to others. Anger may also be displayed in facial expression, bodily set, tone of voice, action, and manner of action, as well as in ways less easily discernible. Any of

---

4 We should, of course, distinguish between a report that is based on ignorance and a report of *a state that is based on ignorance*; for instance, if I report that I believe that Aristotle was born in Athens, and my belief is based on false assumptions, my report is not undermined.

51

these, and especially action, may also help to indicate what one is angry about. In addition to the manifestations of anger, one of the chief indicators of what a person is angry about is what he has reason to be angry about (or what he has reason to be angry about, given his attitudes). Where any of these indicators fails to square with the first-person report, then there is reason to question that report, sincere or not sincere.

I think I have said as much as I need to say in support of BC in particular; and I rest my case, not on any single example but on the entire discussion. Further support will come from showing how BC contributes to the analysis of being angry about a fact. For if the analysis proves on the whole to be a plausible and a useful one, this consideration should overcome any minor qualms the reader may have regarding one or two of the examples offered in support of BC.

It is obvious that BC alone does not provide a complete analysis of being angry about a fact. But together with another requirement to be introduced in the next section, it does constitute the *basic* analysis not only of being angry about a fact but also, mutatis mutandis, of being upset, pleased, or sorry (etc.) about a fact.

HOW TO FIND OUT WHAT YOU ARE ANGRY ABOUT – THE HARD WAY

Anger is a *negative* factive emotion. Therefore, when S is angry about the fact that p, S not only believes that p but also wishes it hadn't been the case that p. There is some redundancy in this formulation, in that 'hadn't been' implies that it was indeed the case that p, at least according to S. To avoid that redundancy I have recommended the formula *wishes it not be the case* that p. Because what S believes is the contradictory or at least the contrary of what S wishes, we can say that S's wish is *frustrated*. Wish-frustration may be defined as a state in which one simultaneously *wishes it not to be* the case that p yet *believes that it is* the case that p. (Since reference to 'the fact that p' presupposes that S's belief is true, the wish is frustrated in reality as well as "in thought"; but at this stage I am concerned only with frustration "in thought.") It is not implied that the wish *preceded* the belief: The wish may have come later than the belief or developed at the same time.

What is causing S to be angry is the belief and the wish in

52

combination; it is, in other words, the wish-frustration that is causing S to be angry. *Anger always arises from wish-frustration, if it is anger about a fact; or, granting that the factive emotions are primarily about facts, as urged in Chapter 2, if it is anger about anything.* The same holds for all the negative factive emotions we have considered.

Where the *positive factive emotions* are concerned, we may speak of wishing it to be the case that p – where this is understood to be compatible with saying both that it is the case that p and that S believes that it is. Thus, when S is pleased (etc.) about the fact that p, then S *wishes it to be the case* that p. And, just as we may say that the negative factive emotions arise from wish-frustration, we may say that the *positive* factive emotions arise from wish-*satisfaction* – a state in which one simultaneously *wishes it to be the case* that p and *believes that it is* the case that p.

We might try to fill out the analysis by adding to the Belief Condition (BC) a parallel *Wish Condition* (WC) as follows:

(WC) If S is angry about the fact that p, then S's wishing it not to be the case that p is sufficient for S to be angry, given some existing conditions that are not themselves sufficient for S to be angry.

Unfortunately WC, though true, does not give us what we want. For the conjunction of BC with WC does not ensure that S's believing that p works, so to speak, in conjunction with S's wishing it not to be the case that p, to make S angry; that is, it does not ensure that the belief and the wish are parts of the *same* sufficient condition. We can easily repair the gap, however, by replacing BC and WC with the following single requirement, which shall be called the Belief-Wish Condition (BWC):

(BWC) If S is angry about the fact that p, then S believes that p and wishes it not to be the case that p; and the conjunction of
    (1) S's believing that p,
    (2) S's wishing it not to be the case that p, and
    (3) some other existing conditions
is sufficient for S to be angry – where no two of these three conjuncts are jointly sufficient for S to be angry.

ad hoc?

BWC holds, mutatis mutandis, for all the negative states listed in Table 2.3. For the positive states, it holds if the 'not' is deleted after 'wishes it' and 'wishing it.' In referring to BWC henceforth I shall understand 'angry' to be replaced by the predicate under discussion; and I shall understand the 'not' to be deleted, where one of the 'positive' predicates is under discussion.

BWC helps us to decide what S is angry about in cases of the following sort. Suppose that Sam is angry about (F_1) the fact that the fellow in the neighboring apartment plays the violin every evening. Among the *grounds* on the basis of which Sam is angry about F_1 are (F_2) the fact that the walls are so thin that any loud activity next door prevents Sam from sleeping, and (F_3) the fact that Sam has to go to work every day at 6:00 A.M. (He is angry about F_1, it would be natural to say, "because of" F_2 and F_3.) Now it might be held – correctly, I think – that in such a case Sam has three beliefs (corresponding to F_1, F_2, and F_3, respectively), each of which satisfies the earlier requirement BC. Given only BC, Sam might be angry about F_1 or about F_2 or about F_3; or he might be independently angry about any two or even all three facts, just as in the earlier example Daddy was independently angry about his car's being laid up and about Junior's having ruined the Hong Kong shots. We need the stronger requirement BWC in order to decide which of these facts, if any, Sam is angry about. BWC requires that we ask, for instance, 'Does Sam wish not to have to go to work at 6:00 A.M.? And is this wish sufficient for him to be angry, when conjoined with his belief that he has to go to work at 6:00 A.M., and so on?'

BWC gives us the *basic* analysis of the negative and positive factive emotions. It appears that it holds without exception for each of those listed in Chapter 2: If there are exceptions, I have not found them. Indeed, aside from certain complications that will be noted, it gives us all that we need in order to decide what fact or facts a person is angry (etc.) about: In other words, it gives us a complete set of truth conditions for sentences of the form 'S is angry (etc.) about the fact that p.'

First complication. It should be noted that some factive emotions are neither negative nor positive. These include surprise, amazement, and astonishment. In place of a "pro-attitude" such as a wish they involve *expectation*: They involve something like wish-frustration, namely, the frustration of expectation. A further type of emotion, *disappointment*, involves wish-frustration along with expectation-frustration.

John is surprised (about the fact) that the plane arrived on time.

54

This is so only if the plane's punctuality was at the time he learned of it *contrary to his expectations*. It may be too strong to say that at that time he expected that it would *not* be punctual. I would be surprised if a huge meteorite were to fall in the path of my car in downtown St. Louis; I would be surprised by the falling object and further surprised *that it was a meteorite*. But it would be problematic to say that I had expected that no meteorite would fall in the path of my car. For one thing, I could not enumerate all the specific types of things whose fall in the path of my car would surprise me: Do I nevertheless have specific expectations regarding each of these? I shall say that the fall of a meteorite, or the punctuality of the plane, is contrary to one's expectations, though there need be no *specific* expectation to the contrary. If S is surprised (amazed, astonished, disappointed) (about the fact) that p, then at the time S came to be certain that p,[5] that p was contrary to S's expectations.

Suppose that John is surprised (about the fact) that the plane arrived on time, because the airline had a reputation for being unpunctual. Two facts are cited; but one is the basis of an expectation, the other is the surprising fact, which is contrary to this expectation. Here is a more interesting example. Morgan was surprised because (a) the sherry he was drinking was an amontillado, and (b) the sherry he was drinking was light-bodied. Which fact was he surprised about? He may have been surprised about the fact that (b), his reason being (a); or he may have been surprised about the fact that (a), his reason being (b). It all depends on which was the basis of his expectation and which contravened the expectation.

Second complication. Many of the factive emotions, particularly negative factive emotions such as anger and indignation, are set off from others by their relatively specialized causal structures. For one thing, there is more to be said about the *beliefs* one must have, if one is to be angry about a fact. Generally, the sorts of things one gets angry about are actions, or consequences of actions, of *other persons*. If S is angry about the fact that p, then S believes not only that p but also that some agent – in standard cases a person or persons other than S – by act or omission brought or helped to

---

5 Which may predate the time S came to know that p, for S might first have been certain, for instance, for inadequate reasons. But only with the onset of knowledge could S be described as being surprised (about the fact) that p.

bring it about that *p*. We do occasionally speak of people as being angry about *their own* actions or about the "actions" of animals or even inanimate objects or forces. Yet these exceptional attributions seem strained: so much so that one feels a strong temptation to say that someone who is angry with himself must see himself as if he were another person; and that someone who is angry with an animal or an inanimate object is regarding it as if it were a person.[6]

Moreover, what a person is angry about is something perceived as, and taken to be, thwarting (or attempting to thwart) one's interests or as threatening (or attempting to threaten) one's self-esteem – a "conspicuous slight," as Aristotle puts it. (At times we speak of people as being angry about actions affecting only the interests or self-esteem of *another*; but in such cases we are inclined to think of the subject as "identifying" with that other person.) Thus, given our ordinary expectations, we would be perplexed by a friend's report that she was angry about being given a large inheritance, say, or a friendly greeting. For how could *that* be seen as hurting her interests? How could *that* threaten her self-esteem? We would probably seek out background information that might make it all plain. Were we fully convinced, however, that she did not see the inheritance (or greeting) as hurting her interests, and so on, then we would have little recourse but to doubt her report. What we would *not* do, I submit, is conclude that she was angry about the inheritance, though "inappropriately" so. Cognitions of the sort I am discussing seem to be required not just for "normal" or "appropriate" anger but for the label *angry* to be applicable at all.

The causal structure for *indignation* would include, in addition, a belief that it is (putting it roughly) *unjust* that *p*. If Sam is indignant that his neighbor plays the violin every evening, then Sam wishes him not to. But this "wish" of Sam's must not be based entirely on considerations of *interest*, whether his own or another's; it must also be based on the unjustness of what his neighbor does, and thus caused by the belief or judgment that it is unjust that his neighbor plays the violin every evening. If moral beliefs play no role in shaping his attitude, Sam is not *indignant* but at most *angry* or

6 It is raining as I write this, and a friend of mine claims to be angry about the fact that it is raining. He doesn't believe in Jupiter Pluvius, but I am inclined on other grounds to think that at the moment he must see "the world" as conspiring against him.

resentful about the fact that his neighbor plays the violin every evening.

On the other hand, for many of the words listed in Table 2.1, the basic analysis of emoting about a fact is adequate without specialized amendments of the sort required, for instance, for 'angry' and 'indignant.' Among these are 'glad,' 'sad,' 'unhappy,' and 'upset.' For those such as 'anger' and 'indignation' that do require specialized structures, BWC provides at least the framework for further analysis. By amending BWC in the ways indicated, namely, by adding more beliefs and perhaps wishes as requisite causes of anger, we should be able to obtain a complete set of truth conditions for sentences of the form '*S* is angry about the fact that *p*.' The same appears to hold for any of the factive emotions. One can easily see how BWC thus amended may be thought of as *a rule for generating formal insights* into anger. A computer program exploiting the rule might yield responses such as the following:

What are you angry about?
My lawn.
What is it about your lawn that makes you angry?
Hardly anything has grown on it.
So you're angry about the fact that hardly anything has grown on your lawn. Who's to blame?
The fellow who sold me that new type of weed killer.
You're angry at the fellow who sold you that new type of weed killer?

Third complication. Although BWC provides insights into the *causes* of anger, it does not tell us what *effect* these causes must have on a person, if he is to be said to be *angry* about a fact. It seems uninformative to say merely that the effect is *anger*. Some psychologists would say that *physiological arousal*, particularly autonomic (sympathetic) arousal, must be produced. Clearly, physiological arousal is not enough. For one thing, we distinguish being "angered" by some action threatening to one's interests or self-esteem from being (merely) "upset" by such an action, although physiological arousal is typical of either state. I doubt if arousal is even necessary to anger. What is important, I believe, is that a certain *action tendency* be produced: roughly, one aimed against the interests or self-esteem of the agent one takes to be responsible for whatever it is one is angry *about* – with allowances, however, for repression or displacement.

Aristotle's definition of anger emphasizes this element. Anger, he wrote, *is*

> . . . an impulse, accompanied by pain, to a conspicuous revenge for a conspicuous slight directed without justification towards what concerns oneself or towards what concerns one's friends (felt towards some particular individual, not man in general).

This element is crucially important in typical *predictive* uses of the concept of anger. For one thing, it would permit us to add further responses to our artificial intelligence program, such as the following:

> I guess your anger makes you feel like doing something nasty to the fellow who sold you that new type of weed killer.

Fourth complication. Suppose that Sam believes he has to go to work every day at 6:00 A.M. and wishes not to go to work every day at 6:00 A.M. Suppose further that because Sam does not have his wish in this matter, his wife is upset; and because she is upset, she cannot pay proper attention to her driving. Finally, her inattentive driving causes Sam to be angry. It could be argued that in such a case Sam's wish–frustration over having to go to work at six is, given the intermediate linkage described, sufficient for Sam to be angry. Yet he is not angry about anything more than the fact that his wife is not paying proper attention to her driving.

What is required is a formula that will filter out all such counterexamples yet admit intermediate linkages of the right sorts. (Similar formulas are required by the belief-want analysis of intentional acts and the causal theory of perception.) But the problem of constructing a formula that will admit all and only the right sorts of intermediate linkages does not seem to me at all crucial to the acceptability of the basic analysis. Once we have narrowed the gap in our analysis to this problem of intermediate linkages, the analysis can no longer be fundamentally threatened by exotic counterexamples. They become tools, rather, for hacking out the needed formula.

Fifth complication. Any sentence of the form '*S* is angry about the fact that *p*' presupposes the corresponding sentence '*p*.' Thus it

58

might not be true that S is upset about the fact that p, even though the Belief-Wish Condition is satisfied: for it might not be true that _p_. But there is more to this complication than meets the eye, as I shall try to show in the section that follows.

KNOWLEDGE: THE MISSING LINK

It is common to suppose that when we say of someone that he is, for instance, angry about this or that, we are saying something, essentially, just of him. One extreme form this supposition takes is the doctrine, criticized above, that what a person is angry about is just a matter of how he feels. If it so happens that the form of words we use to describe his state carries a presupposition that what he is angry about is true or is a fact, this is incidental.

Yet there appears to be no form of words that entails everything that is entailed by sentences of the forms 'S regrets that p' and 'S is angry about the fact that p' minus only the entailment (or presupposition) of 'p.' Neither English nor any of the (few) European languages I have looked into has such a form. To avoid commitment to the truth of 'p' one either speaks with the understanding that one is adopting the subject's point of view, as in novels and psychiatric case studies; or abandons sentential complements altogether – both 'that' clauses and 'about' phrases with (explicitly or implicitly) sentential objects, such as the following:

· The fact that Dewey was elected
· Dewey's having been elected
· Dewey's election

Instead of using the sentence 'Dewey was elected' as a complement of the emotion term ('regrets,' 'is angry'), one may instead use it to specify a belief that is causally linked to the emotion:

> 'Smith is angry because he believes that Dewey was elected.'
> 'The cause of Smith's regret was his belief that Dewey was elected.'

We can show the presupposition of 'p' to be something more than an incidental matter – a linguistic surd or brute fact, so to speak – if we can show that when someone is angry about the fact that p, the causal structure underlying S's anger includes not only the elements specified in BWC (e.g., Smith's believing, or taking it to be a fact, that Dewey was elected) but also the actual event or state of affairs, if any, referred to by the gerundized version of '*p*' (e.g., by the phrase 'Dewey's having been elected'). But this is at least suggested, as I shall explain, by the argument of the previous chapter, in which I tried to establish that if *S* is, for example, angry (etc.) that *p*, then *S* not only *believes* but *knows* that *p*. (The arguments are applicable to any of the factive emotions.) In the discussion that follows I shall assume as a further "requirement" the following Knowledge Condition (KC):

(KC) If *S* is angry (etc.) about the fact that *p*, then *S* knows that *p*.

KC is important to my present purpose for the following reason: In recent years several *causal* analyses and *reliability* analyses of propositional knowledge have been proposed (e.g., Goldman 1967; Skyrms 1967; Unger 1967; Dretske 1971; Nozick 1981). These differ from one another in various details. But all, or almost all, are agreed on one point, namely, that *if* S *knows that* p *then* S *would not have believed that* p *if it were not the case that* p. Not all philosophers are agreed even on this point, needless to say; but analyses that hold at least this much have won wide acceptance. The use to which I am able to put this point can only strengthen its credibility.

Given a causal or a reliability account of factual knowledge, the Knowledge Condition has the consequence that if Smith regrets that Dewey was elected or is angry or delighted (about the fact) that Dewey was elected, then Smith's regret (anger, delight) is causally or at least counterfactually tied to the state of affairs, *Dewey's having been elected*. To generalize: When *S* is angry about the fact that *p*, the state of affairs referred to by '*p*' (in gerundive form) is indeed a part of the causal structure underlying *S*'s anger. To be more specific, it is necessary, under the conditions, for *one* of the elements in the causal structure delineated in BWC, namely *S*'s belief that *p*; that is, *S* would not have believed that *p* if it were not the case that *p*. This means that, aside from cases in which *S* is independently angry about several matters, the state of affairs referred to by '*p*' is causally necessary, under the circumstances, for *S* to be angry.[7] For example, before his discovery that Junior had ruined the Hong Kong shots, Daddy would not have been

---

7 I assume that '*x* is necessary for *y*' and '*x* is sufficient for *y*' are each transitive relations, even if '*x* is a cause of *y*' and '*x* causes *y*' are not.

angry had it not been the case that his car would be laid up at the shop. It can also be shown that the state of affairs referred to by 'p' is causally *sufficient* for S to be angry, even where S is independently angry about several matters at once; though with some complications, especially where 'p' is future-dated.

Thus it is a mistake to suppose that to say of someone that he is angry about this or that is just to say something of him, with at most an incidental implication that what he is angry about happens to be the case. We are also saying something about "external" events or states of affairs, in asserting that certain causal relations obtain between them and certain states of the subject. This conclusion squares with common sense and ordinary language. Common sense says that when you are angry or delighted about, for instance, Dewey's having been elected, Dewey's having been elected *affects* you in some way; namely, *it makes you angry*, or it *delights you*. You are angry *because* Dewey was elected. If you *regret* that Dewey was elected, then Dewey's having been elected is the "cause" or "source" of your regret.

Obviously it is useful to think in terms of counterfactuals or causal connections that link a person's demeanor to the world. This is of particular importance in social emotions such as anger, indignation, and gratitude. If such linkages went unrecognized, the behavioral expressions of these emotions would lose their power to *reinforce* the corresponding types of behavior in others. Social harmony requires learning what has made another grateful, so that one might repeat it; or what has made another angry, so that one might *not* repeat it.

In this matter alone my analysis of the relation between anger and what it is about has two advantages over Kenny's claim that such ostensibly causal expressions must be understood as having a special noncausal sense: It is consistent with the systematically causal locutions used to express that relation and hence obviates the need to explain away their causal implications; and, more impressive than this negative virtue, it actually explains why we use such locutions to express that relation.

SOME CONSEQUENCES OF ACCEPTING THE ANALYSIS

1. It is sometimes suggested that the central or standard cases by which the concept of anger is to be understood are cases in which

61

a person is not just angry, but angry *about* something. Thus it is not just a contingent fact that anger is, at least in standard cases, anger *about* something. Even the stronger suggestion may be made that it is conceptually impossible that someone be angry yet not angry about something. If my analysis is assumed, then either suggestion entails that it is not a contingent matter that anger arises from certain causes rather than others: namely, that when someone is angry, he has (at least in standard cases) a wish-frustration that stands in a certain causal relation to his anger, as specified in BWC. The stronger suggestion, that it is conceptually impossible that someone should ever be angry yet not angry about something, has on my analysis the following interesting consequence: that there can be no such thing as an anger agent. Nothing, neither a drug nor anything else, can induce anger without the help of some wish-frustration, as specified in BWC. This, of course, would make the questionnaire experiment described earlier a conceptual impossibility.

Whatever we say in the case of anger, it is clear that one is never *indignant* without being indignant about something. This is not to say that one can at the time always *state* what one is indignant about, beyond saying "some injustice or other." The point can be expressed in terms of the proposed analysis, as follows: What may symptomatically appear to be indignation actually is not, if it is not generated by the right causal structure, including an agency belief and (roughly) an injustice belief; otherwise what we have is at most anger or resentment, or perhaps mere displeasure with some state of affairs. Thus there can be no drug that acts as an *indignation agent*. I am not quite so sure, however, what to say about a state that symptomatically resembles *anger* but is not produced by an agent-caused wish-frustration. The aboutness of anger seems to me to be a very important semantic feature, for without it anger would be little more than a strange psychosis that strikes people inexplicably from time to time, saddling them with ugly desires and bizarre physiological disturbances. Because symptomatic anger that is not about something is so rare, however, we do not have a contrasting term that enables us to say, "This is not true anger but at most _____." Were such cases to become common, I should think they would soon acquire a name of their own – most likely a name that clearly marks the state as a disease. Then we should be able to say without reservation that no one is *angry* unless he is angry about something.

2. Just as, in general, there are alternative true descriptions under which someone's act is intentional – 'He flipped the switch,' 'He turned on the light,' and so on – so there generally are alternative true specifications of what someone is angry about. To return to an early example, even supposing that Sam is not *independently* angry about several things at once, we might still say that he is angry about "the fact that his neighbor plays the violin every evening," "the fact that he is prevented from sleeping every evening," "the fact that he is unready for work at six in the morning," and so on. One of the virtues of the present analysis is that it permits us to explain this. For what we have in this case are three frustrated wishes; namely, that the neighbor not play the violin every evening, that Sam not be prevented from sleeping, and that Sam not be unready for work. These wishes presumably all derive from one "basic" wish, perhaps the last of those mentioned or perhaps some other wish of Sam's, such as not to risk being fired from his job. That is why I say that although Sam is angry about several facts at once, he is not *independently* angry about several facts at once. It is plain that there are many parallels to be explored here between my analysis of being angry (etc.) about something and the belief-want analysis of intentional action.

3. The proposed analysis does not conflict with the claim that emotion sentences satisfy certain criteria of *intentionality* (sometimes thought to mark off mental states from physical). It does, however, have the interesting consequence that the intentionality of emotion sentences is *derivative* from the intentionality of sentences that ascribe beliefs and wishes. For example, the sentence 'Smith is angry about his being the last person invited to the party' is intentional on one of the three criteria (namely, nonsubstitutivity) originally proposed by Chisholm (1957). But this sentence is true only if a certain sentence of the following form is true: 'Smith is M because he believes that he is the last person invited to the party and wishes not to be the last person invited to the party.' But any sentence of this form would be intentional on the nonsubstitutivity criterion, even if 'M' were replaced by some blatantly physical predicate; for the nonsubstitutivity is introduced by the belief and wish clauses. Thus, even if the criterion were successful in distinguishing mental

states from physical, it would not show that *being angry* is per se a mental and not a physical state.[8]

4. According to the analysis here proposed, our presumed ability to discover in many cases what an individual is angry about is an ability to secure at least implicit knowledge of the causal structure underlying his anger. Given our further ability to recognize that this or that act or physiological condition is a manifestation of anger, we can know at least implicitly that the act or condition had a certain causal structure. What the proposed analysis does is to convert our implicit knowledge of this causal structure into explicit knowledge. Thus in a way it adds to our explicit knowledge of the causes of particular acts and psychogenic physiological conditions.

SUMMARY

I claimed in the preceding chapter that wish-frustration and wish-satisfaction are involved in the negative and positive factive emotions, respectively. We now have a clearer idea *how* they are involved. If, as I have argued, BWC gives us the basic analysis of the factive emotions, then words such as 'upset,' 'sad,' and 'glad' designate certain *effects* of wish-frustration or wish-satisfaction. To say that human beings are *susceptible* to being in such states as being upset, being sad, and being glad is to say that wish-frustration and wish-satisfaction sometimes have certain effects on human beings. Words designating factive emotions with relatively specialized causal structures – for example, 'angry,' 'indignant,' and 'proud' – designate effects of particular *types* of wish-frustration or wish-satisfaction – particularly those arising from a certain *source*, such as (roughly) another's ill will. To say that human beings are *susceptible* to being in these states is to say that wish-frustration and wish-satisfaction sometimes have these *special* effects on human beings.

---

8 This conclusion is vitiated, however, if we grant that as a matter of definition to be angry is to be angry about something. For in that case, it may be argued, 'Smith is angry' is true just in case *some* intentional sentence of the form 'Smith is angry about x' is true; hence Smith is angry just in case he is in a mental, nonphysical state described by at least one of these intentional sentences. In any case, if being angry is a disposition to acquire *desires*, etc., the advocate of intentionality is back in business: for now we should have to cope with the intentionality of sentences about desires.

4

Epistemic emotions

In this chapter I examine the formal structure of epistemic emotions. I do so with a particular interest in discovering structural features that will help us to explain the several resemblances between these emotions and belief. Most important, we want to understand the *functional* resemblance. To be afraid, terrified, or worried that *p*, one needn't believe that *p*; one needn't think it probable that *p*; one might even (as we shall see) think it *im*probable that *p*. Yet someone who is afraid, terrified, or worried that something is so typically acts as if he "assumes the worst," namely, that it *is* so. Similarly, someone who is *hopeful* that *p* typically acts as if he "assumes the best" – again, that it *is* so. And yet he needn't believe it so, or even probably so; he might even think it probably *not* so. I shall try to explain this in terms of the causal structure of epistemic emotions. Most of the discussion will concern *fear* in particular. But much of what I shall say applies equally well to other epistemic emotions, as I shall try to make clear at the end of the chapter.

There is sometimes thought to be a special obstacle to causal analyses of the epistemic emotions. The "cause"-"object" distinction briefly noted at the beginning of the preceding chapter seems to have special importance for states classified under the traditional heading of "forward-looking" emotions. Kenny elaborates Wittgenstein's admonition to "distinguish between the object of fear and the cause of fear" (1953:135), as follows:

There are . . . cases where the object of an emotion is quite clearly distinct from its cause. This is most obviously so in the case of the forward-looking emotions, such as hope, dread, and excited anticipation, where the object is something which is as yet in the future and therefore cannot be the cause of the emotion which belongs to the present. (Kenny 1963:72)

It is easy to find examples that seem to support a distinction between "the cause" and "the object" of fear, despite the vagueness and ambiguity of both terms. I fear an explosion: that is, I am afraid that there will be one. Yet there need be no past explosion that is the cause, or even *a* cause, of my fear. And if some explosion were to occur in the future that "bears out" my fear or makes what I fear "come true," *that* explosion will not have been the cause, or even *a* cause, of my antecedent fear, because future events and states do not cause present or past events and states. Apart from this, what I had feared – the so-called object – was not *that* explosion, the individual event that makes my fear come true, but *any old* explosion within certain typically vague parameters, such as in the shed, caused by a fault in the kerosene heater, within the next few weeks. There is no actual event, past, present, or future, that is identical with what I fear.

That these are not very serious challenges for a causal analysis becomes evident once the alleged forward-looking character of these emotions gives way to an implication of *uncertainty* – whether about matters past, present, or future. Such uncertainty, contemporaneous with one's fearing, provides a most plausible candidate for a cause or causal condition. In addition, the implication of uncertainty will help account for the nonreferential reading of 'an explosion,' when we ask what the implied uncertainty is uncertainty *of.* I do not know whether anyone has ever asserted or implied the identity between "the object" and "the cause" of fear that Wittgenstein denied, but abandonment of that fancied identity is no setback for a causal analysis.

We encounter a far more serious problem for a causal analysis when we ask, Just what is *caused by* the uncertainty that is implicit in fearing? It would be nice if we could say, on the model of our analysis of the factive emotions, that the uncertainty causes one to be *afraid*, or to be in a *state of fear*, which in turn has such and such effects. The difficulty is that even though uncertainty sometimes does cause people to be afraid or in a state of fear, many of our less visceral, less "emotional" fears seem to involve no such state. Ordinarily it would be ludicrous to characterize a person who is afraid that it will rain or that his rosebush was harmed by the frost as "afraid" or "in a state of fear." Fear of an explosion may or may not involve such a state.

The uncertainty implicit in fearing will be shown to be of a special kind: *nondeliberative* or *external* uncertainty, uncertainty that is not due merely to one's being undecided among alternative actions. One *fears* something only if such uncertainty produces a special *motivational* effect. To describe the effect in very broad terms, one

66

is motivated to take things into one's own hands: to increase the scope of one's control over the world, to decrease the scope of one's helplessness. Typically, fearing motivates people to avoid vulnerability, so that even if what they fear *proves true*, they will have salvaged what is importantly at stake.[1] One carries an umbrella, lest it rain; one boards the rescue boat, lest one go down with the ship; one climbs a tree, lest one be mauled by the bear. One seems to be acting as if one *believed* one's fears to be true – as if one *assumed*, and not merely *feared*, the worst. Therein lies the functional resemblance to belief. Therein, too, lies the key to the causal structure of fearing: a structure that nonvisceral fears, such as (typically) *being afraid that it will rain*, have in common with our more formidable fears and terrors.

BROADENING THE PURVIEW

I believe that all fearing is "propositional," that all fears are fears that something is (or: was, will be) the case. The formula 'S fears (is afraid) that *p*' is comprehensive enough, or more precisely empty enough, to embrace the vaguest of so-called objectless fears, for even at that extreme one at least fears that there is *something bad* that one doesn't yet know about – something bad that is (was, will be) the case. This fact, if it is a fact, is of some importance. To fear that something is so quite plainly involves cognitive and attitudinal states. If all fear involves fearing that something is so, then all fear involves such states. And this fact would seem to be of some importance.

Many of the expressions used to specify what a person fears or is afraid of are essentially nothing more than abbreviated sentences. Thus, to be afraid of an explosion, a reprisal, or a third world war is just to be afraid that *there will be* an explosion, a reprisal, or a third world war. Gerundive nominalizations, as in 'She is afraid of slipping on the ice,' are evidently produced by transformation of an embedded sentence: The more explicit form would be 'She is afraid that she will slip on the ice.' But 'Joe is afraid of a (particular) dog' is grammatically unlike 'Joe is afraid of an explosion,' on the

---

1 Just what one is motivated to do depends, we shall see, not on what one fears to be so but on *why* one fears it; more specifically, on what I shall call one's *attitudinal reason* for fearing it.

most natural reading of each. In the former, the nominal expression 'a dog' does not seem, at any rate, *merely* to abbreviate some sentence. Even here, however, if Joe is afraid of a dog then there is a dog such that Joe is afraid that *it will harm him.* (He needn't, however, *believe* it will. See below.) Again, 'She is afraid of sledding on the ice' is grammatically unlike 'She is afraid of slipping on the ice.' The former is neither equivalent to nor even entails 'She is afraid that she will sled on the ice.' Nevertheless it entails something like 'She is afraid that if she sleds on the ice then she will be harmed (or something bad will happen).' In sum, there is reason to think that even if we set our sights only on the formula '*S* fears (is afraid) that *p*,' the scope of our analysis is really broad enough to encompass all that is essential to the concept of fear.

EPISTEMIC AND ATTITUDINAL REASONS

There are, as I have indicated, certain cognitive and attitudinal conditions a subject satisfies, if he is truly said to fear that something is so. First, if *S* fears or is afraid or terrified that *p*, then *S cares* whether or not *p*: More specifically, *S* wishes it not to be the case that *p* ('wishes that not-*p*,' for short). And second, if *S* fears (is afraid) that *p*, then *S is neither certain that* p *nor certain that not-*p. For example, if Joe fears that there will be an explosion, then Joe wishes it not to be the case that there will be an explosion, or to put it less awkwardly, he wishes there to be no explosion. But Joe is not certain there will be no explosion, nor for that matter is he certain that there will be an explosion.

I should note that there are some conventional uses, especially of the first-person forms 'I fear that *p*' and 'I am afraid that *p*,' that do not carry the entailment of noncertainty – for instance, 'I am afraid you will have to find another job.' But these are plainly parasitic on a use that does carry this entailment. It should be pointed out, too, that '*S* fears that *p*' does not entail '*S* believes that *p*.' In fact one may even fear that something is so while believing it is *not* so. A man may fear that his draft lottery number will be among the next one hundred called, although he recognizes that the probability that this will occur is only one in ten thousand. Because he believes the lottery to be (technically) a fair one, he believes, and perhaps is almost certain, that his number will not be among the next one hundred. Still he fears the worst; he may even be terrified of it. Finally, this and other examples make trouble for the widespread view that fearing always involves believing that one is *in danger*, believing that (something) is *dangerous*, or believing that *there is a danger* of (something) happening.

I have already noted that in the case of the epistemic or "uncertainty" emotions, there exist two distinct kinds of *reasons* that a person may have for emoting that *p*. Moreover, these correspond to the two logical conditions I have cited, namely, the wish and the uncertainty. For example: Tom is afraid that Sarah will be at the party. Why? Because she often comes to these parties. But why is Tom *afraid* she will be there? Because he and she had parted with bad feelings. The answer to the first "Why?" states what I have called an *epistemic* reason of Tom's for being afraid that Sarah will be at the party, that is, Tom's reason (or one of his reasons) for *not being certain* that Sarah will *not* be at the party. (It may, of course, be more than that: a reason for *believing that she will* be at the party.) The answer to the second "Why?" states an *attitudinal* reason of Tom's for being afraid that Sarah will be at the party: Tom's reason (or one of his reasons) for *wishing* that she *not* be at the party. A sentence states an *epistemic* reason of S's for fearing (being afraid, being terrified) that *p*, if and only if it states a reason of S's for *not being certain* that not-*p*. A sentence states an *attitudinal* reason of S's for fearing that *p*, if and only if it states a reason of S's for *wishing* that not-*p*.

Some other examples may help make the distinction vivid:

· He is afraid it will rain, because there are dark clouds overhead. (*epistemic*) / because he will get wet (or: he doesn't want to get wet). (*attitudinal*)
· I'm afraid there is someone in the next room, because I thought I heard footsteps. (*epistemic*) / because our conversation may be overheard. (*attitudinal*)
· He was terrified there were demons in the house, because the candle flickered out. (*epistemic*) / because they do the Devil's work. (*attitudinal*)

From what has been said, we should expect that something may qualify in either of two ways as a reason for fearing that something is so, but in only one way as a reason for regretting that something is so. Any of the examples given in Chapter 2 may be used to illustrate this; but I prefer to introduce one more, in order to clarify certain points.

Imagine that a man is about to play Russian roulette. Since the pistol to be used has six chambers, only one of which is loaded, he may not believe that the pistol will go off when he pulls the trigger, and he may, perhaps reasonably, believe that it will not go off. Yet we should not be surprised to find him afraid that the pistol will go off. His reasons might plausibly be, first, simply the fact that *one of the six chambers is loaded* – and thus the pistol may go off when he pulls the trigger. And second, the fact that *the pistol is pointed at him* – which is why its going off matters so much to him.

I think we must agree that these are indeed *reasons for being afraid* that the pistol will go off. We might also agree that these are good and sufficient reasons: that he *has reason to be afraid* that the pistol will go off. (Note that he has reason to be afraid that the pistol will go off, only if he has both reason to believe that it may, or at least might, and reason to wish that it would not.) The point I wish to emphasize, and which the grotesque example was designed to bring out, is that a reason for being afraid that something is so need not also be a reason for believing that it is so. The fact that exactly one of the six chambers of a pistol is loaded is not, by itself, a reason for believing that the pistol will go off when the trigger is pulled; it is, if anything, a reason for believing that the pistol will not go off. (With one's life at stake, of course, it may be wise to be conservative: to act just as one would act if one believed that the pistol would go off.) A reason for being afraid that something is so may sometimes be no more than a reason for believing that it might be so, that is, for believing it possible that it is so. I should explain that I understand a person to believe it possible that something is so, just in case he believes that it might be so, *for all that he can say for certain*; and thus, just in case he is not entirely certain that it is not so; or, what I believe comes again to the same thing, just in case he has even the slightest doubt that it is not so.

To summarize the main points made in this section: S fears (or is afraid, terrified, or worried) that *p* only if S wishes that not-*p* and is neither certain that *p* nor certain that not-*p*. It is not required that S *believe* that *p*, only that S believe that there is a *possibility* that *p*. But this is not to say a *danger* that *p*. (The concept of danger, I might add, seems tied to the notion of what is *worthy of being feared*. To use the concept in the analysis of fearing would be circular; moreover, the belief that there is a danger seems too sophisticated to be a condition of fear in general.) S's epistemic and attitudinal reasons for fearing that *p* are, respectively, S's reasons for being less than certain that not-*p* and for wishing that not-*p*.

To wish that not-*p* while uncertain whether *p* or not-*p* does not add up to fearing (being afraid) that *p*. I wish to be able to finish this page tonight, am not certain whether I will be able to or not, but am not *afraid I won't* be able to. For one thing, I may on the contrary be *hopeful I will* be able to finish the page tonight. Being hopeful that not-*p* has thus far the very same logical preconditions as fearing that *p*. Yet the two states are, I think it is clear, not mutually compatible: If I am hopeful I'll finish the page, then I am not afraid I will not. (I may *hope* I will, though I am afraid I will not, but that is quite a different matter.) What makes the two states incompatible? There must be a further precondition for each, the one incompatible with the other.

If we take the "certainty" emotions as our model what we should find is that only when the wish and the uncertainty interact to produce some further *state* can a person be said to fear that something is the case. But what state would this be? A state of *fear*? But it is simply not true that whenever someone fears or is afraid that something is so, he is *afraid*, or in a *state of fear*. Fears range wider than fear. Someone who is afraid that it is going to rain or who fears that his rosebush was harmed by the frost is unlikely to be in such a state that we can say of him truly, "He is afraid," or "He is in a state of fear."

The *state of fear* appears to have been a complex evolutionary experiment, perhaps universal among mammals, involving physiological (especially autonomic) arousal, the riveting of attention, readiness for flight, and a disposition to flee. Such a state might also be termed the *flight-arousal syndrome*. Since mammals of other species clearly exhibit the syndrome, one might say that they are subject to (states of) *fear*. It is more problematic to hold them to be subject to *fears*. I am less reluctant to speak of a mouse or a cat as *afraid*, or in a *state of fear*, than I would be to speak of it as afraid *that it will be hurt* or as fearing *that the dog will attack it*. It may sometimes be useful to attribute such fears in explaining as well as in predicting the animal's behavior, but it is important to do so with an understood *qualification*: that the attributed fear contents do not have anything *remotely* like the set of inferential connections such contents would be expected to have in a standard attribution, particularly an attribution to ourselves or to most other human beings. Thus one should not suppose a mouse to infer from its being hurt that it may be *wounded* or otherwise *injured*, or even that *a mouse* is hurt; or to infer from the dog's attacking it that a living thing attacked it, or that something larger than a normal-sized grapefruit attacked it. Nearly all inferences, even many that are central to our own conceptual networks, must be bracketed in explanations and predictions of mouse behavior.[2]

It does seem natural enough to speak of a mouse as fearing, or afraid of, another animal, or some physical object, or the like. But this usage can be explained – and justified – simply as follows: The mouse's perception of the presence or proximity of the object *causes* the mouse *to be in a state of fear*. (Here 'causes' may be glossed either dispositionally or occurrently.) Perhaps the same is implied when a human being is said, for instance, to be afraid of a dog. But it is also implied that she is afraid *that the dog will hurt her* (if she gets too close). This latter implication is more problematic, as argued above, when it is a mouse or a cat that is said to be afraid of a dog. As long as the implication is suspended, however, I can see nothing problematic about saying, of a member of a languageless species, that it has, say, a fear of people, or a fear of automobiles, or a fear of loud noises.

In human beings the flight-arousal syndrome is a frequent accompaniment, and perhaps product, of a particular category of fears, namely, fears of violent death or injury to oneself. (Perhaps we might include in this category many of the phobias, such as fear of heights, fear of snakes and spiders, and even stage fright.) Fortunately, the syndrome seems virtually confined to this category, whereas the bulk of our fears do not fall under this category. Our fears range as wide, given the right circumstances, as our wishes; and our wishes range as wide, given the right circumstances, as the indicative or subjunctive sentences we can construct. The state of fear is far too special a phenomenon to serve in the analysis of fearing that *p*.

(In addition, even if we could *distinguish* fearing that *p* from being hopeful that *p* by saying that in the one case it is *fear* that is caused whereas in the other it is something else – *hopefulness*, perhaps? – this would not explain why fearing that *p* is *incompatible* with being hopeful that *p*.)

---

2 I was even less tolerant of mouse fears in Gordon (1980).

On the other hand, all fears, whether or not they put us into a state of fear, have a similar *motivational effect.* Whether one is terrified that a burglar has just entered the house or merely afraid, as we say, that it is going to rain, one acquires a similar tendency to action. The similarity between, say, phoning the police in the former case and taking an umbrella in the latter case is a structural one, and not immediately obvious. It comes fully to light only when we have examined the peculiar structure of epistemic and attitudinal conditions that give rise to "fear-motivated" action. I propose now to define that structure.

THE MOTIVATIONAL EFFECT

It might be thought that what fearing motivates one to do, or try to do, is to prevent one's fears from "coming true." (This appears to be the view of Kenny [1963:92] and also that of Armstrong [1968:182].) Fearing that p, one tries to bring it about, and if possible to ensure, that it is not the case that p. But this common impression is a mistaken one.

Certainly the examples I have presented do not support the generalization. Fearing that a burglar has entered the house, I cannot suppose that there might be something I could now do to prevent this from *having* happened. I phone the police and try to exit by the back stairs, not to prevent the burglar's having entered but to prevent certain consequences that might ensue if indeed a burglar has entered. Again, fearing that someone is in the next room, I might, for example, lower my voice, so that even if it is true that someone is in the next room, our conversation will not be overheard. Afraid that it will rain, one takes an umbrella, not to prevent it from raining but to bring about conditions in which it is false that *if it rains one will get wet.* Afraid that Sarah will be at the party, Tom decides not to dissuade her from going, but not to go *himself,* so that it will be false that *if she will be at the party then they will have an embarrassing confrontation.*

The key to the motivational effect of a fear is the *attitudinal* reason for that fear. For in order to predict how fearing that p will motivate a person to act, we must know (as I shall argue) why he cares whether p or not-p and, specifically, what reason or reasons he has for wishing that not-p. Now a fully explicit statement of a reason of S's for *wishing that not-p* will generally implicate a *second* wish

73

of S's. Such a statement will have the form "If p then q," where S wishes that not-q. For the examples I've given, the explicit statements of the respective attitudinal reasons might run as follows:

· If Sarah will be at the party, then (because Sarah and I parted with bad feelings) I will have an embarrassing encounter. (I wish *not* to have an embarrassing encounter.)
· If it will rain, then I will get wet. (I wish *not* to get wet.)
· If there is someone in the next room, then our conversation may be overheard. (I wish our conversation *not* to be overheard.)
· If there are demons in the house, then I will be the Devil's victim. (I wish *not* to be the Devil's victim.)

Although there are apparent counterexamples to be considered, the above examples suggest that the right account of what fearing motivates is as follows:

· If S fears (is afraid, is terrified) that p, and an attitudinal reason of S's is that if p then q, then S is motivated (e.g., tries or at least desires or wishes) to bring about conditions in which it is *false* that *if* p *then* q.

Note that if S *successfully* brings about such conditions, then S's attitudinal reason or reasons for fearing that p will no longer obtain. There are instantiations where, because of conflicting desires, S does not go so far as to *try* to bring it about that not (if p then q), hence only *desires* to bring this about. And there are other instantiations where S, assured that it would not be *possible* for S to bring it about that not (if p then q), might be said not to *desire* this outcome but only to *wish* it. (E.g., one fears it will rain, where no shelter or protection is available.) But at least we may attribute to S a "pro-attitude" such that if it were satisfied or carried out into successful action, then conditions would be such that it would be *false* that *if* p *then* q.

Fear-motivated action might accordingly be characterized as *vulnerability*-avoidance. Action is taken such that even if one's fear "comes true" or (in more general terms) what one fears to be so *is* so, one will have salvaged what is importantly at stake. By taking an umbrella with me when I go out I bring it about that conditions are not such that if it rains then *I will get wet*. Of course, this does not guarantee that I will not get wet from any source: Armed against the rain I may nonetheless get doused, rain or no rain, by an errant lawn sprinkler. What my action does is merely to *sever the connection* that according to my attitudinal reason, pres-

74

ently obtains between the contingency that it will rain and the contingency that I will get wet.

It may be urged that I have focused unduly on fears concerning matters over which one has, and typically knows one has, no possible control, for example, meteorological events and past or present events that are already faits accomplis, such as a burglar's *having* entered the house. What of the engineer's fear that the bridge will collapse? Couldn't it motivate her to take measures to reinforce it so that it will not collapse? Couldn't the fear that one's car will rust motivate one to have it rust-proofed?[3] One might think that in at least some such cases, contrary to what I have been saying, a person is motivated by fear to prevent what is feared from coming true: that S's fearing that p at least *may* motivate S to bring it about that not-p. But close attention to such examples reveals what I shall later term the *optionality* of the motivating fears. Thus what motivates the engineer to reinforce the bridge is her fear that *it will collapse if she doesn't* reinforce it – or do something else to prevent its collapse. What motivates me to have my car rustproofed is my fear that *it will rust if I don't* have my car rust-proofed – or do something else to prevent its rusting. One is moved to avoid the *residual* uncertainty and vulnerability, that which obtains if one *doesn't act*; and to avoid it, one *acts*. (This point is developed in the section on "Nondeliberative Uncertainty.")

Aside from vulnerability avoidance, there is no type of action that our fears *characteristically* motivate, or that constitute their "natural expression." No general description such as "flight" will do. Even when the content of the fear is specified, no characteristic action can be specified. Fearing it will rain, one may take an umbrella, remove the clothes from the line, postpone an outing, or move one's campsite – not to mention the more outlandish possibilities – depending on one's attitudinal reason or reasons for fearing it will rain. Given certain typical general attitudes or values, of course, there are typical attitudinal reasons for certain fears – for fearing, for example, that a burglar has entered the house. But even here one's action may depend on whether it is one's life or merely one's property that is thought to be at stake. It is in any case the

3 These examples are from Davis (in press), responding to Gordon (1980).

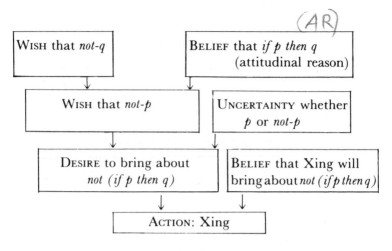

(AR)

WISH that *not-q*	BELIEF that *if p then q* (attitudinal reason)

WISH that *not-p*	UNCERTAINTY whether *p* or *not-p*

DESIRE to bring about *not (if p then q)*	BELIEF that Xing will bring about *not (if p then q)*

ACTION: Xing

Figure 4.1.

attitudinal reason, not the content of the fear, that delimits the motivation.

The *state of fear*, on the other hand, does characteristically involve a tendency to flee, as I asserted earlier. The flight response that arises in a state of fear is probably a genetically coded fixed action pattern "designed" for immediate protection against relatively primitive sources of physical harm. It may sometimes happen to coincide with our fear-motivated attempt to render the attitudinal reason false; for instance, afraid that we are being followed, we run, on the one hand, as a manifestation of our state of fear and, on the other hand, because we believe that by doing so we avoid certain consequences that might ensue if indeed we are being followed. But all too often our nonrational flight response conflicts with our fear-motivated action or desire; for example, afraid that the dog will attack, we try to do as we have been taught, "Stare at the dog and don't run away." But our fearing that the dog will attack may induce a state of *fear*, which disposes us to run away and makes it difficult to do otherwise. Similarly, the infantryman, fearing himself surrounded, is motivated to surrender but panics and tries to run. In such cases our fears both motivate vulnerability-avoidance and at the same time create a Frankenstein state that impedes such action.

The block diagram in Figure 4.1 depicts in a general way the structural relationships that obtain when one's fearing that something is so motivates one to action, and as a result one acts accordingly. The arrows represent causation. It is to be understood that in any actual instance the causation would occur against a background of causally relevant conditions not represented in the diagram. To bring out the structural relationships, I designate various states in a simplified way; for example, '*S*'s wishing it not to be the case that *p*' is rendered '*wish* that not-*p*.' Finally, *epistemic* reasons are not represented at all in the diagram.

why?

Any of our examples may be plugged into the diagram, as follows:

1. *p* = It will rain.
   q = I will get wet.
2. *p* = Sarah will be at the party.
   q = I will have an embarrassing encounter.
3. *p* = There is someone in the next room.
   q = Our conversation will be overheard.
4. *p* = There are demons in the house.
   q = I will be the Devil's victim.
5. *p* = A burglar has entered the house.
   q = Some of my possessions will be taken.

Note that the same structural relationships hold whether one is brought to a *state of fear*, as is likely in examples (4) and (5), or not, as is likely in (1). We do make the following distinction, however. In example (1), I take my umbrella "for fear that it will rain" or "because I am afraid it will rain"; but I do not take it "out of fear." Only if I am brought to a state of fear do I act out of fear. And even then, I am not acting out of fear unless the state of fear causes (or at least is a causal condition of) the action. I *flee* from the dog out of fear: but if I stand my ground and stare, I probably do not do so out of fear, even if I do so for fear that (because I am afraid that) otherwise the dog would attack me. Thus, there appears to be a distinction between *fear-motivated* action and action *done out of fear*. Where the same action is both fear-motivated and done out of fear, we seem to have a case of causal overdetermination.

What I find most intriguing about the structural relationships represented in the diagram is the relationship between fear-motivated action and the attitudinal reason (AR). Fear-motivated action is aimed at so modifying conditions that the AR underlying the fear – or at least one of the AR's, if there are several – is made false. What happens, then, when someone takes such action and

77

believes he has thereby modified conditions in this way? He ceases to hold a belief on which his very fear was founded, and unless there are other props supporting his fear, he ceases to fear. For example, since I have now taken my umbrella, for fear that it will rain, I no longer believe that if it rains I will get wet. Unless I also had *other* attitudinal reasons for fearing it would rain, I cease to be afraid that it will rain. I may continue to be *uncertain* whether it will rain or not, and perhaps I believe it will rain: but I am no longer *afraid* it will rain. This property fears have of being, under optimal conditions, *self-extinguishing* should be evident from an examination of the diagram. With minor additions – an arrow from the ACTION box at the bottom to the BELIEF box at the top, and a negation indicator – the causal relationships depicted constitute a negative feedback loop, a system switched off by its own output.

What is more interesting is that a fear may extinguish itself even before the fear-motivated act has actually been carried out. For, even before the act has been carried out, I may expect it to be, and that is all that is required to eliminate the attitudinal reason. Because I now expect I shall have my umbrella with me, I no longer believe that if it rains I will get wet. Because I expect to avoid the demon-haunted house, I no longer believe that if indeed there are demons in the house, I will be the Devil's victim. Here the feedback loop is closed even before the fear-motivated act has been carried out.

The diagram thus helps to explain an interesting empirical finding. The social psychologist Richard Lazarus found that the *physiological stress* produced by "threat," that is, danger, is significantly reduced or eliminated when people think they are able to *cope* with the threat (1966). (This finding had an influence on the procedures used in training astronauts.) Given some very minor empirical assumptions, we have only to apply what was said in the previous paragraph – which is itself no more than an unpacking of some implications of the conceptual scheme represented in the diagram – and the experimental result follows as a logical consequence. The main empirical assumption we need to make is one the experimenters tend to make also, namely, that the stress being measured in these experiments is stress that has resulted from fear and would not have existed without the fear. (The only other assumption we need is that the subjects are at least minimally rational; for example, they do not believe a certain thing will happen if they believe they are going to prevent it from happening.) Because the results were as could have been predicted from the analytic scheme I have presented, given only these plausible empirical assumptions, the analytical scheme has had some experimental confirmation.

There is, I believe, a simple key to the overall structure of fear motivation. The key is the fact that not just any uncertainty fills the UNCERTAINTY role in our diagram: Deliberative uncertainty is excluded. If the only reason I am not certain whether *p* or not-*p* is that I am *undecided which of two or more action alternatives to choose*, then I cannot be said to fear (be afraid) that *p*. The ship's captain is *certain* he will drown *if* he stays with his rapidly sinking ship. And he is certain he *will not* drown *if* he boards the rescue vessel. But he is undecided whether to stay with his ship or board the rescue vessel, and therefore uncertain whether he will drown or not. However, if what I have maintained is correct, the captain cannot be said to be *afraid he will drown*. (Nor can he be said to be "afraid he will drown *if* he stays with his ship": for he is *certain* of that.) Similarly, a tennis player may be undecided whether to put a lot of effort into winning or to put only moderate effort into it, knowing, however, that if he does the former he will win whereas if he does the latter he will lose. He is not *afraid he will lose*. Again, I am not *afraid I will drop the vase* if I am sure I will drop it if I don't put it down immediately and (of course) sure I won't drop it if I do put it down immediately.

Let's consider a slightly different situation, in which the worst option has an uncertain outcome. Suppose again that the captain is deliberatively uncertain whether he will stay with the ship or board the rescue vessel, and certain he will not drown if he does the latter. But he is not certain of the outcome if he remains with his ship: It just might not sink, and so he might not drown after all.

Figure 4.2 may help to make it clear how the various contingencies are related. Is the captain afraid that *he will drown*? Perhaps, if he were to take it for granted that he will not take the option of boarding the rescue boat. But if, on the other hand, he is deliberatively uncertain whether to remain with his ship or to board the rescue boat – if both of these are live options – then he is not afraid that *he will drown*. What motivates him to board the rescue boat,

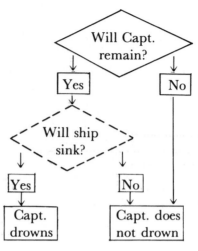

Figure 4.2.

then? He doesn't board the rescue boat for fear that he will drown: but he may do so for fear that *otherwise* he will drown, or simply for fear that his ship will sink. For these contingencies – that his ship will sink, and that he will drown *if* he remains with it, *if* he doesn't board the rescue boat – are *nondeliberatively* uncertain.

The answer to the question 'Will the ship sink?' is not up to him; it is a matter of *nondeliberative* uncertainty, as the dotted lines in the diagram are meant to indicate. The captain may fear that the answer to this question is "Yes," his attitudinal reason being that the "Yes" branch leads to the outcome he wishes to avoid, namely, that he drowns. Of course, this reason is predicated on the assumption that the *deliberative* question 'Will the captain remain with his ship?' is answered in the affirmative. Were he to opt for the negative, the attitudinal reason underlying his fear would be undermined; thus he is *motivated* to opt for the negative, that is, to board the rescue boat.

The captain may also be said to be afraid that *he will drown if he remains with his ship.* This is an example of what may be called an *optional fear*: One fears that one's Xing (where Xing is a live option) would have a particular outcome. An optional fear motivates one *not* to take the option mentioned. The captain, afraid he will drown *if* he remains with his ship, is thereby motivated not to remain with his ship. I am afraid I will drop the vase if I don't put it down

80

immediately; therefore I will be motivated to put it down immediately.

In everyday speech, where contextual understandings often make explicitness unnecessary, we sometimes delete the option clause when describing what is in fact an optional fear. For example, 'The captain boarded the rescue vessel because he was afraid he would drown' – which is to say, afraid he would drown otherwise, that is, if he didn't board the vessel, if he stayed with his ship. Or again:

> Why did you put the vase down?
> Because I was afraid I would drop it.

That is, afraid I would drop it otherwise, or, if I didn't put it down.

Until the optionality of these fears is made explicit, they appear to be counterexamples to the thesis that fearing motivates, not the avoidance or prevention of what is feared to be so, but the avoidance of vulnerability *in the event one's fears prove true*. By putting the vase down I do make it false that I will drop the vase. But what motivated my putting it down was my fearing that I would drop it *if* I didn't put it down. And this *conditional* isn't made false by my action. By putting the vase down I see to it that the antecedent option clause is not satisfied, and thus that the following argument is not a sound one *even if* the conditional, which I fear to be true, should happen in fact *to be* true:

> If I don't put the vase down I will drop it.
> I don't put the vase down.
> Therefore, I will drop it.

We may sum up by recalling what was said about the role of the attitudinal reason in explaining what a fear will motivate one to do. One is motivated to act in such a way that the attitudinal reason underlying the fear is made false. In the ship's captain example, the fear is that his ship will sink. The AR would be that if his ship sinks, then he will drown. The AR is represented in the decision flow-chart (Fig. 4.2) by the sequence shown in Figure 4.3. The motivational effect of the captain's fear is thus simply *to avoid any optional path containing this sequence*.

In our example we supposed that the captain had an alternative, namely, boarding the rescue boat, which offered a sure escape from drowning. What if, instead, the best of the alternative paths also contains a nondeliberative question on which serious consequences are thought to hinge? To keep complications to a minimum, sup-

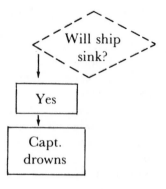

Figure 4.3.

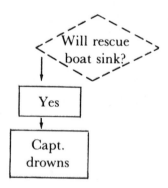

Figure 4.4.

pose the question is 'Will the *rescue boat* sink?' and the "Yes" branch leads once again to the outcome "Captain drowns."

It may or may not be true that the captain *fears* that the rescue boat will sink, or that he will drown if he boards it. Remember from our earlier discussion that to wish that not-*p* while uncertain whether *p* or not-*p* does not add up to fearing that *p*: Not all dire possibilities are fearful. But suppose that indeed the captain does fear that the rescue boat will sink, and that he fears it because if the boat sinks then he will drown. In that case the captain will be motivated to avoid any optional path containing the sequence shown in Figure 4.4, as well as the sequence indicated in Figure 4.3.

To explain what a person actually does in such a case of conflicting fears, we introduce quantitative language, at least of an ordinal sort: We speak of one fear as "stronger" than the other, and we say, for

82

instance, that the captain was *more afraid* of his ship's sinking than he was of the rescue boat's sinking, or more afraid he would drown if he remained with his ship than he was afraid he would drown if he boarded the rescue boat. This would explain why the captain actually boarded the rescue boat.

Perhaps we may say that insofar as the ordering of the captain's fears is *rational* it will correspond to the ordering of his subjective probabilities. But in that case we must acknowledge that one's fears are often not rationally ordered. Many people are greatly afraid of dying in a plane crash who have little or no fear of dying in an automobile crash, although they know the statistics and would even wager accordingly, for instance, when it comes to paying for insurance against accidents of one sort rather than the other.

Suppose, finally, that the captain thinks he has no options whatever. He is trapped on his ship. Or he has only the alternative of attempting to swim, where he is certain to drown if he did so. What action is then motivated by his fear that the ship will sink? Here I think we must characterize his motivation conditionally, namely, "If there is another option – a way of avoiding the sequence beginning 'Will ship sink?' – then take it." (Of course, typically one would also be motivated to avoid alternatives that make drowning a *certainty*.) Such conditional motivation would at least explain the captain's attempt to *discover* new options. It might also explain the captain's fantasies of rescue.

It is easily confirmed that in each of the epistemic emotions – such as, being terrified, being worried, and being hopeful – the requisite uncertainty is always *nondeliberative* uncertainty: One is not uncertain just because one is *undecided*. In the virtue of this restriction these emotions bear a suggestive resemblance to the *factive* emotions, such as regretting, being angry, being embarrassed, being sad, or being pleased. For in the latter the requisite *certainty* appears never to involve *deliberative* certainty. By deliberative certainty I mean certainty that depends on one's being *decided* on a certain course, on having one's mind set on doing (or not doing) something. Such certainty would concern only a future contingency, whereas typically one has regrets or is pleased or angry about what already is the case. But consider regrets, and the like, about the future. I may regret (or be pleased, etc.) that *you* are set on doing a certain thing, and that *you* are going to do that thing. But can I regret or be pleased that *I* am set on doing something, that in fact *I* am going to do something? Here some fine distinctions are required. Bill's mind is set on ordering a diet dessert (when the waitress comes by). He cannot regret that he is going to do this. He may regret that he *has to*, but that would concern only the *circumstances* of his decision. He cannot be *pleased* (much less delighted) that he is going to do this, although he may be pleased that he is (or will be) *able* to do this: whether in respect of his having the *strength of will*, or in general the requisite *psychological* ability. His certainty on these matters, however, does not depend on his being *decided*, for example, that he shall have sufficient strength of will. A parallel distinction must be made for fear. Bill might fear that when it comes time to order he will lose his resolve to order a diet dessert. He is uncertain, therefore, whether he will keep his resolve or not, and thus whether he will order the diet dessert or not. But that is not because he is now uncertain whether *to* keep his resolve or not, or uncertain whether *to* order the diet dessert or not. The underlying uncertainty, once again, is not deliberative uncertainty.

SUMMARY

In fearing that something is so, one is motivated *to reduce nondeliberative uncertainty regarding issues that matter, issues one cares about.* Which specific actions one is motivated to take depends not on what one fears to be so but on *why* one fears it; more specifically, on one's *attitudinal reason* for fearing it. For this tells us what it is *about* what one fears that *particularly matters*: It tells us what one cares about. One is moved to take action – or, at least, to look for action to take – that *insulates* those issues that matter from the nondeliberative uncertainty one has about some other issue. In this way, one takes things into one's own hands, increasing the scope of one's control over the world, decreasing the scope of one's helplessness.

This explains the functional resemblance to belief. Even though one might think it highly improbable that what one fears to be so *is* so, one acts *as if* one believed, indeed knew, it would rain, *as if* one knew the ship would sink, *as if* one knew one would be mauled if one didn't escape from the bear – as if what one fears to be so *were* so. One is motivated to behave *conservatively*. Thus we should not be surprised to find that the farmer who fears a drought sets out pipes in preparation for irrigating the land. And if irrigation and similar measures are unavailable, we should not be surprised to find the farmer seeking *some* way to make the success of his harvest less dependent on rain. Finally, if he despairs of finding a way to insulate his crops from the whims of nature, we should expect to find him "feeling bad" – as if he *knew* not only that there would be a drought but also that, as a result, his crops would fail.

The *hopeful* farmer may not actually believe, for example, that it will rain, and he in any case falls short of being certain that it will. And yet the *wish* that it will rain gives him a tendency to act *as if* he were certain, indeed as if he knew, that it would rain and that as a consequence his crops would flourish. (Hopefulness may be thought of as a mild form of *wishful thinking*.) His hopefulness gives him some motivation to leave matters in the lap of the gods, to take no measures to increase the scope of his own control over the things that matter. He has at least some inclination to rest content: to "feel good" even in the absence of measures that decrease his vulnerability. This is not to say that in fact he will not take such measures. One may be hopeful of something, yet by nature or on principle act prudently or conservatively nevertheless.

We now have a clearer idea why fearing, worrying, being terrified, and being hopeful may be considered *epistemic* states. One may have epistemic *reasons* for fearing, worrying, being terrified, or being hopeful; one's fears, hopes, and worries may be said to be "confirmed" or "borne out"; and, most important, one who fears, and so on, that *p* is motivated to act and to feel as one would if one believed, indeed knew for certain, that *p*.

5

The trivialization of emotions: James and Schachter

Suppose it to be common knowledge that one is *angry* only if one is in a state caused by a certain type of wish-frustration – roughly, a "perceived slight." Suppose further that some of the ways in which anger typically *manifests itself* are also typical manifestations of certain *other* emotions as well. The same type of effect may have any one of a variety of emotional causes or even entirely non-emotional causes: Certain diseases or drugs might produce it. The effect may be an "external" manifestation at least as readily apparent to others as it is to oneself, such as the lowering of the eyebrows. Or it might be one that is more readily perceived by oneself, such as a general arousal of the autonomic nervous system, or what people sometimes call (with doubtful accuracy) the "rush of adrenaline."

On what basis would a person – the subject himself or someone else – decide whether the effect is a manifestation of anger, of some *other* emotional state, or of no emotional state at all? If the various emotions discussed in Chapters 3 and 4 are differentiated largely by their respective causal structures, then one's answer should depend, at least in large part, on *what one believes to be causing the state of which the effect is a manifestation*. If one believes that state to be caused by what the subject perceives to be a slight, then one will be inclined to "label" the lowering of brows or the "rush of adrenaline" a manifestation of *anger*; if one believes the state to be caused by uncertainty of the sort described in Chapter 4, then one is more likely to label it a manifestation of *fear*; finally, if one is quite sure that it is caused, say, merely by an injection of some substance that operates without the intercession of the subject's beliefs or "perceptions," then one will be quite sure that it is *not* a manifestation of anger or fear or any other emotion. If, for example, one suspects that the "rush of adrenaline" was caused "directly" by an injection of adrenaline, then one would be likely to withhold any *emotional* characterization of the arousal.

An experiment with results that conformed to these expectations thus would seem to confirm the general view espoused in earlier chapters of this book. An experiment reported by Stanley Schachter and J. E. Singer (1962), often regarded as a paradigm of experimental social psychology, did in fact produce such results.

I was heartened when I first read their study a number of years ago: Empirical confirmation of a philosophical thesis is as exciting as it is rare. But I soon discovered that Schachter, at least, had a different idea. Rather than taking the results to support certain conclusions about our common knowledge about emotions, for example, that each is characterized in large part by a certain type of situational cause, Schachter thought the experiment to show "common knowledge" to be radically mistaken. Anger is *not* (among other things) a state caused by a "perceived slight." It is rather a state caused by the *belief* that one is in a state that is caused by a slight. What counts chiefly is what one *believes* to have caused one's arousal. For Schachter, the actual differentiation into a variety of emotions is basically a product of "suggestion" triggered by physiological excitation. The confusion is compounded by an ambiguity in the notion of a cognitive theory of emotions. Schachter's theory is often considered, especially by psychologists, to be a "cognitive" theory (sometimes, a "cognitive-arousal" theory). But it will be seen that there are two quite distinct types of cognition – two types of *belief* – that must be distinguished. Corresponding to these are two antithetical types of "cognitive theory" of emotions. Reconciliation is possible, I shall suggest in this chapter, at the end of the section "The Inflammation Experiment," but only if due care is given to whether one is theorizing about the nature of emotional states or theorizing about the causes of emotional "feelings."

Schachter takes his own theory to be a refined, cognitivized version of William James's theory of emotions.[1] Each is a theory that, as its author acknowledges, denies to emotions the causal roles assigned them by "common sense." There are serious flaws in each theory, as I shall try to show, if it is viewed as a theory of the nature of the emotions. Yet each may have some merit, I shall suggest, when judged as a theory of the causes of emotional "feel-

---

1 The view I am attributing to James is sometimes characterized as the "James–Lange" theory of the emotions. Lange was a Danish physician who put forward a theory largely similar in its essentials to that of James. See James and Lange (1885).

87

ings": But when seen only in *that* role the two theories are not inconsistent with the commonsense view but at most an elaboration of it.

I begin with James. "Our natural way of thinking," James notes, posits such causal chains as the following:

- Because we have met a bear we are frightened, and because we are frightened we tremble or run.
- Because we have learned that we have lost our fortune we feel sorry, and because we feel sorry we weep.
- Because we have been insulted we grow angry, and because we are angry we strike.

In general, the common view is "that the mental perception of some fact excites the mental affection called the emotion, and that this latter state of mind gives rise to the bodily expression" (1884).

According to James, common sense has it backward. *Emotions do not cause the so-called bodily expression of emotion* that often accompanies them: the weeping, trembling, grimacing, quickening of the pulse, running, striking, and so on. James replaces this causal tie with its converse: *The bodily "expression" causes the emotion.* From another's trembling, perspiring, and running away we may indeed infer fright – as the likely *effect* of these occurrences, not as their likely *cause*. From weeping, and the like, we may infer sorrow, but again, not because sorrow often leads to weeping but because weeping often leads to sorrow. No longer may we attribute a scowl or a reddened face to anger: An "angry scowl" would in fact be at most an anger-*inducing* scowl, and a man "red-faced with anger" would be a man whose flushed face may be *causing* him to be angry.

The commonsense and the Jamesian pictures of cause-effect relationships may be diagramed, respectively, as in Figure 5.1, with the arrows pointing from cause to effect. These are the two conflicting pictures, according to James – except that, to keep things in perspective, I have included in each scheme something James did not discuss or even mention: the cognitive and attitudinal intermediaries "Takes U as insult by S, cares about being insulted by S, etc." For James a state such as fear, sorrow, or anger becomes a mere *epiphenomenon*, an inconsequential by-product of physiological excitation. Like any theory that identifies emotions with a kind of "feeling," James's theory robs emotions of what I have called *causal depth*. In either case, emotions come to be cut off, in large part, from the rich network of causal connections discussed

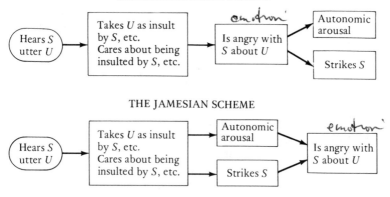

Figure 5.1.

in the preceding chapters.[2] With this ablation, emotion concepts would seem to be of little value in the explanation and prediction of behavior.

On the face of it the Jamesian "revolution" is preposterous. The so-called *expression* of emotion causes the emotion? The actions that emotions supposedly *motivate* cause the emotion? What conceptual convolutions could have led James to such a radical inversion of the commonsense view? Here is the imagination experiment that provides the principal "data" that James appeals to as his supporting evidence:

> If we fancy some strong emotion, and then try to abstract from our consciousness of it all the feelings of its bodily symptoms, we find we have nothing left behind... and that a cold and neutral state of intellectual perception is all that remains. (1884)

James explains that his argument chiefly concerns the "coarser" or "stronger" emotions, such as those in which there is a pronounced "wave of bodily disturbance." The "bodily symptoms" of these emotions include "facial expressions," peripheral physiological effects such as weeping, flushing, trembling, and quickening of the pulse, and the "voluntary" muscular responses characteristic of certain emotions – running away, striking or other types of physical aggression, and so on. James asks us to imagine feeling

---

2 Although in the case of Schachter, curiously, emotions depend on the subject's *believing* that there is such a network.

some emotion and then to *subtract in imagination*, to "imagine away," all the feelings of the so-called bodily symptoms – to imagine *not feeling* what our muscles are doing, the state of our cardiovascular system, and so on – and finally to examine *what remains of the original image of our emotional feeling*. All that will remain, James maintains, is a perception (or memory) of the "object," a cognition that is entirely lacking in emotional "coloration."

James understood this experiment in "subtracting in imagination" to be a modest substitute for a more respectable type of empirical investigation. Ideally, we should be studying the effects of *real-life* subtraction. That is, we should be investigating people who suffer a pathological deficit in bodily feedback, people with a seriously impaired capacity for perceiving (feeling) what their bodies are doing. Would such people also have an impaired capacity for experiencing emotion? If so, that would be, "if not a crucial test, at least a strong presumption, in favor of the truth of the view we have set forth; whilst the persistence of strong emotional feeling in such a case would completely overthrow our case" (1884). At the time there had been no systematic studies of such cases. And so James settles for an imagination experiment. (Schachter cites some recent clinical studies that appear to support James's prediction of impaired emotional capacity.)

A HISTORICAL EXCURSION

A brief glimpse at the historical background will help to show the significance James took his imagination experiment to have. In *The Expression of Emotions in Man and Animals*, published in 1872, Charles Darwin tried to explain the various, mostly involuntary physiological changes, especially in the facial and skeletal muscles, that constitute the so-called expressions of emotions. (These he thought to be, for the most part, the inherited remnants of once useful actions.) His work led others to broader investigations of the characteristic physiological "accompaniments" of the emotions, including the internal visceral phenomena that were not part of the outer "expression" of emotions. Still, these studies accounted for what were believed to be mere *accompaniments* or at best *manifestations* of the emotions, leaving untouched "the emotions themselves." It was left to the introspectionist psychologists, most notably Wundt and Titchener, to investigate "the emotions themselves." For these psychologists the scientific study of, for instance, *fear itself* consisted in the systematic description of one's feelings – or, more broadly, one's "state of consciousness" – when one is afraid. The assumption was that "fear itself" – that inner state of which the physiological expressions are manifestations – is just a certain feeling or state of consciousness.

In contrast to the biological studies of physiological "expressions" and "manifestations" of the emotions, however, the introspectionists' attempts to chart the nuances of emotional feeling were guided by a tightfisted empiricism that eschewed all *explanation*. In a stance that was mimicked by the most extreme of the twentieth-century behaviorists, the introspectionist psychologist expressly took care not to penetrate beneath the surface of his "experience." To William James, such descriptive studies offered no insight or understanding; they were as tedious as "verbal descriptions of the shapes of the rocks on a New Hampshire farm" (1890:chap. 25). And he asked, "Is there no way out from this level of individual description in the case of the emotions? I believe there is a way out, but I fear that few will take it" (1890:chap. 25).

James's "way out" was to take this tack: Perhaps when one experiences any of the variegated emotional feelings that psychologists had been trying to capture in their taxonomies, what one feels – in a perceptual sense of "feel" – is precisely those peripheral physiological phenomena that Darwin and the biologists had been studying. This hypothesis would demand a change of perspective. No longer could the study of emotional feelings be regarded as a special science, insulated from our general theory of man as a biological organism; and no longer could the physiology of emotion be thought of as a study of certain inessential *accompaniments* of the inner life. Physiology replaces phenomenology at center stage. Not the study of the midbrain and the "old cortex" but the study of the skeletal muscles and the viscera – and especially of those phenomena that constitute the so-called expressions or, more broadly, the "manifestations" of the emotions. For it is precisely our perception of these peripheral phenomena that gives us the peculiar "feel" of various states. Unfortunately, as we shall see, James inherited from the introspectionists the assumption that the "fear itself" is just a certain feeling or state of consciousness. Hence his view, no less than theirs, deprives emotions of causal depth.

91

Suppose, then, that James is right about the results of his imagination experiment: It is indeed our feelings of the bodily "symptoms" that *emotionalize consciousness,* that imbue it with emotional quality. Without them, there would be only "a cold and neutral state of intellectual perception." To use a term currently in vogue among philosophers, "what it is like" to experience anger, fear, sorrow, or intense joy is accounted for by what it is like to undergo certain types of physiological excitation and certain types of (voluntary or involuntary) muscular response.

Taken by itself, I suggest, this is a very interesting idea; I shall say more about it later in this section. James's reasoning from this point on appears to be roughly as follows:

1. It is our feelings of the bodily "symptoms" of emotions that imbue our consciousness with emotional quality.
2. Our feelings of the bodily symptoms of emotions are caused by, and do not cause, the bodily symptoms of emotions.

Therefore:

3. The emotional quality of consciousness is caused by, and does not cause, the bodily symptoms of emotions.

This argument seems a sound one, given, of course, that we accept premise (1). Premise (2) is highly plausible: It is the rapid heartbeat that causes the "feeling" of rapid heartbeat, not the other way around. And so – if we assume (1) – it is indeed the physiological "expression" of, say, fear, and the actions motivated by fear, that account for "what it is like" when we fear something.

But James does not want to stop there. He wants to say that

4. Our *emotions* are caused by, and do not cause, the bodily symptoms of emotions.

But to warrant that conclusion he needs a premise that ensures that *if (3) then (4).* That is, he needs to assume that if a state *feels like,* for instance, anger then it *is* anger. Or, in other words:

5. An emotion (such as anger) *is* nothing but a particular (emotional) quality of consciousness.

It is important to see that one may accept James's theory that it is a person's bodily reactions to a perceived stimulus – the rise in

92

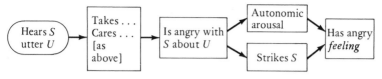

Figure 5.2.

blood pressure, the jaw-clenching, the movement of the arm as it strikes the provoker – that cause him to feel the way he does when he is angry (etc.), and yet maintain also that the bodily reactions are themselves manifestations of an *underlying* state, namely *anger*. Thus one might hold that the perception – together with certain background beliefs and attitudes – causes a state of anger; that this state then causes the bodily reaction; and the bodily reaction in turn gives rise, finally, to the peculiar angry *feeling* one experiences. This might be called the "*Combined* Jamesian Scheme" because it appends James's account of emotional *feeling* to the commonsense picture of *emotion*, as shown in Figure 5.2.

Support for this is particularly strong in the case of fright or fear, for many people report having fled from danger or taken other emergency actions, then feeling fright or fear only after the danger was past. According to the Combined Scheme, it would be intelligible to say that they had fled out of fright or fear, even though the characteristic feeling came later.

James did not consider the possibility of merging his account of emotional feeling with the traditional view of emotion: He took it for granted that a state such as fear or anger consisted in nothing more than the experience of the resultant feeling. James accepted without question the then current assumption that the peculiar "feel" of an emotion *is* the emotion. In fact, he did not seem aware that there was an alternative. More specifically, as he explained in a later retrospective paper, "I myself took it for granted without discussion . . . that the special emotions were names of special feelings of excitement" (1911:225).

This assumption, when conjoined with (1) and (2) above, leads James to what he rightly regards as a radical inversion of "our natural way of thinking about the emotions." It leads to the conclusion that people have been wrong to suppose that the so-called bodily manifestations of anger were really manifestations or effects

93

of anger, and that emotionally "motivated" muscular behavior was indeed motivated by an emotion. For the emotional feeling is an *effect* of these bodily phenomena, not their *cause*. The bodily changes "follow directly the *perception* of the exciting fact, and . . . our feeling of the same changes as they occur is the emotion."

This conclusion, which James frequently represents as *the thesis* of his writings on the emotions, is indeed far more radical in its implications than was the hypothesis discussed in the previous section, namely, that it is the perception of bodily changes that emotionalizes our consciousness. So much is this contrary to our accustomed thinking about emotions that James himself lapses from it at a critical point. For he thinks his hypothesis corroborated by the (alleged) fact that we feed the flames of an emotion when we give expression to it. For example, "Each fit of sobbing makes the sorrow more acute, and calls forth another fit stronger still." Clearly he presupposes here that the more acute "sorrow" created by weeping is not an epiphenomenon but *a state that disposes us to weeping* – as well as, no doubt, to other expressions and manifestations of sorrow. Throughout his lengthy discussion of the aggravating or reinforcing effects of "giving expression" to various emotions, James unwittingly reverts to the accustomed picture of an emotion as the common underlying cause of its various "manifestations." It is no wonder, then, that two of James's critics, the physiologists Sherrington and Cannon, misconstrued his thesis. They found that experimental animals that had been surgically deprived of visceral feedback would continue to "exhibit emotion," for example, in facial expression and vocalization. Therefore, they argued, the animals must have continued to experience emotion. This inference wrongly took James to be arguing that emotion *as commonly conceived*, namely, as the underlying cause of the various "symptoms" of emotions, including facial expression and vocalization, was a product of visceral feedback. On the contrary, James had explicitly denied this; his position was that emotions were *effects*, not *causes*, of these symptoms.

THE ADRENALINE EFFECT

For a number of years the possibility of a real-life test of James's theory of the peripheral origins of emotional feelings absorbed the attention of a number of psychologists. Much of this interest soon

94

focused on the experimental use of adrenaline, a substance secreted by the adrenal medulla and clearly implicated in many of the bodily changes accompanying at least fear and anger. The effects of adrenaline appear to be similar to those of the "sympathetic" branch of the autonomic nervous system: increases in systolic blood pressure and heart rate, for example, as well as other systemic adjustments that according to Cannon and others, equip the organism for strenuous muscular activity; also palpitations, tremor, sometimes flushing and accelerated breathing, with reported feelings of nervousness. Those who have had heavy doses of caffeine will be familiar with many of these same effects.

If the peripheral theory were correct, shouldn't a person who has received an injection of adrenaline report that he feels afraid, say, or angry? No: For if the bodily feelings induced by adrenaline are merely a common denominator of distinct emotional states, even if only fear and anger, the peripheralist would argue that there must be some further bodily feeling or feelings that distinguish these states. The person who has received the injection might well report that he feels a kind of excitement, such as he often feels in fear and anger, but that "something" is missing from the experience. This is indeed the sort of response one often gets in such an experiment, for example, in the early and often cited study by Marañon (1924).

From what has been suggested earlier it would appear that what is missing in the adrenaline experience is really a number of elements: visceral and motor phenomena specialized for various distinct types of emotion, desires or impulses to action typical of certain emotions, the riveting of attention or the clouding of thought, and so on. But aside from the limitations of adrenaline, there is an additional limitation introduced by the experimental situation itself. As Stanley Schachter noted:

Though Marañon does not explicitly describe his procedure, it is clear that his subjects knew that they were receiving an injection, and in all likelihood they knew they were receiving adrenaline and probably had some familiarity with its effects. In short, though they underwent the pattern of sympathetic discharge common to strong emotional states, at the same time they had a completely appropriate cognition or explanation of why they felt this way. This, I would suggest, is the reason so few of Marañon's subjects reported any emotional experience. (1971:3)

The point, as I take it, is not simply that the subjects had an appropriate explanation, but that it was a kind of explanation that

95

made it unnecessary for them to explain their arousal as a manifestation of some emotion. The point is made more explicit by Bertrand Russell, who came to much the same conclusion in the more mundane setting of a dentist's office:

> On one occasion my dentist injected a considerable amount of [adrenaline] into my blood in the course of administering a local anaesthetic. I turned pale and trembled, and my heart beat violently; the bodily symptoms of fear were present, as the books said they should be, but it was quite obvious to me that I was not actually feeling fear. I should have had the same bodily symptoms in the presence of a tyrant about to condemn me to death, but there would have been something extra which was absent when I was in the dentist's chair. What was different was the cognitive part: I did not feel fear because I knew there was nothing to be afraid of. In normal life, the adrenal glands are stimulated by the perception of an object which is frightful or enraging; thus there is already a cognitive element present. . . . But when adrenalin is artificially administered, this cognitive element is absent and the emotion in its entirety fails to arise. (1960:226–7)

Russell and Schachter apparently agree that it is the causal explanation one gives for the bodily symptoms one feels that determines whether they will have the "feel" of *an emotion* or not. Schachter goes even further to suggest explicitly that the particular causal explanation one gives determines whether the bodily symptoms will have the feel of *fear* or of *anger* or of *joy* or whatever. Without presuming to decide whether each of these states has its own physiological idiosyncrasies, he suggests that a massive arousal of the sort induced by adrenaline might, *when complemented by the appropriate sort of causal explanation*, take on the "feel" of fear or anger or joy or some other emotional state. Here I understand Schachter to mean that, even if adrenaline arousal may lack some of the bodily symptoms characteristic of fear, for example, the subject will be likely to overlook the absence of the additional symptoms and not miss them, provided he is sure enough that his arousal is due to a "fearful" stimulus or situation. The same point could be made, I suppose, about symptoms other than bodily symptoms: Even the absence of characteristic impulses, fixations of attention, and so on, might be overlooked if one had a sufficiently compelling arousal *and* a sufficiently compelling explanation of it.

THE SCHACHTER–SINGER EXPERIMENT

Perhaps, then, if subjects given an adrenaline injection could be duped into thinking that their arousal was due not to the injection but, rather, to some typically emotion-arousing situation, the arousal would take on the "feel" of fear or anger or some other emotion. This was the thought behind the experiment of Schachter and Singer (1962).

In that experiment, the injection of adrenaline was disguised as an injection of a vitamin supplement. Although no subjects were told that they were receiving adrenaline, some (the "Informed" group) were given an accurate picture of the physiological "side effects" they would feel. Others (the "Ignorant" group) were not told of any side effects.[3] Those in the latter group, it was thought, would be unlikely to connect up their subsequent feeling of arousal with the injection they had received; they would therefore have to search elsewhere for an explanation.

The experimenters then saw to it that an alternative explanation would be readily available. Some subjects were asked to fill out a routine questionnaire, which in fact asked personal questions designed to offend. To insure that the subject would recognize the situation as a provocation to anger, it was arranged that his "partner," actually a stooge, would appear irate, to the point of tearing up the questionnaire and storming out of the room. Other subjects found themselves in a far more pleasant, though equally "emotional," situation. The subject merely waited in a room cluttered with paper scraps and playthings, with a euphoric partner whose prearranged antics progressed from doodling to flying paper airplanes to hula-hooping.

After being exposed to one or the other of these environments, all subjects were asked to what degree they would describe themselves as "feeling irritated and angry," and also to what degree they would describe themselves as "feeling happy and good." As predicted, the degree of emotion reported depended on the information given the subjects about the effects of the injection. The Ignorant subjects, who had been led to think they would feel no side effects of the injection, rated themselves significantly "angrier" or "happier," depending on the situation, than the Informed subjects – that is, angrier in a situation that seemed to call for anger, happier in a situation that seemed provocative of good spirits.

---

3 Another experimental group, the "Placebo" subjects, is discussed briefly later in this chapter. A fourth group, the "*Mis*informed" subjects, may for present purposes be disregarded.

Finally, subjects injected with an inert substance rather than adrenaline (the "Placebo" group) tended to report relatively little emotion of *either* type. Moreover, objective tests showed relatively little physiological arousal on their part. Thus it appears that, without the help of the injected adrenaline, the situations themselves were not sufficiently "emotional" to have caused significant physiological arousal on their own; and without physiological arousal there was less tendency to report feeling either angry or happy.

Schachter's interpretation of the results is that the Ignorant subjects had mistakenly attributed their arousal to the emotional situation they found themselves in, and therefore perceived the arousal to be an *emotional response* to that situation – one of anger or happiness, whichever was appropriate or to be expected in such a situation. On the other hand, the *Informed* subjects, furnished with a readily available physiological (and nonemotional) explanation for their arousal, would have been less likely to see it as an emotional response to the situation.

Schachter claims that the experimental results support a theory he characterizes as "modified Jamesianism": "for emotion is viewed," he says, "as visceral activity in interaction with cognitive or situational factors" (1971). The theory is Jamesian in that it holds physiological and especially visceral arousal to be a necessary condition of emotional feeling or experience. (Hence the Placebo group reported relatively little emotional feeling.) Here Schachter agrees with James's theory. If *A* is to experience emotion, *A*'s body must undergo such arousal and *A* must *feel* the arousal – that is, perceive it, presumably by interoception rather than, for example, just by *hearing* one's quickened heartbeat.

For James, such felt arousal *constituted* emotional feeling. For Schachter, on the other hand, the "cognitive or situational factors" alluded to above must also be present. To experience fear, for example, one must characterize or label one's situation in a certain way, namely, as of a sort that typically arouses fear, such as one in which one is in danger of being injured or killed. It isn't enough, however, merely to feel arousal at the same time one happens to find oneself in such a situation. Even with a *cognition* (i.e., recognition or belief) that one is in such a situation, one will not experience fear unless one *connects up* that cognition with the arousal one feels. To do this requires a *second* cognition: a recognition or belief that it is one's being (or taking oneself to be) in a situation

98

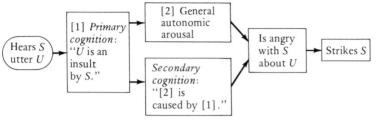

Figure 5.3.

of danger that is causing the arousal one feels. Unfortunately, Schachter makes no explicit distinction between these two cognitions, the one – which I shall call the *primary* cognition – labeling the situation (e.g., as dangerous) and the other, the *secondary* cognition, attributing one's arousal to the situation thus labeled. But it is clear that according to his theory both are necessary for emotional experience.

Not only are both cognitions necessary if there is to be emotional experience, on Schachter's account: It is they that chiefly account for the difference between the experience of anger, the experience of fear, the experience of joy, and so on. Here again, Schachter disagrees with James, who had proposed that the entire spectrum of emotional experience – of "strong" emotion, at least – was produced by distinctive patterns of physiological activity. Schachter, though he allows that there may be some physiological differentiation among, say, anger, fear, and joy, holds that it is chiefly the subject's *cognitions* that determine how he will label his state. Thus the same state of arousal may be variously labeled "anger," "fear," or "joy," depending on the sort of situation the individual believes to be causing the arousal. According to Schachter's theory, then, the typical causal history of anger would be roughly as represented in Figure 5.3.

Although Schachter does not address the issue, presumably he would allow that his "angry" subjects were angry *about* something. They were not angry about the *injection*, of course – the actual cause of their arousal. They were angry about *what they took to be* the cause of their excitation: the intrusiveness of the questionnaire, or something of that sort (Schachter and Singer 1962:391). They were angry about this, despite the fact that (on Schachter's assumption)

99

it *didn't arouse them in the least*! What caused the arousal was the injection; and what caused the reported "anger" (according to Schachter), and also, Schachter claims, corresponding emotional behavior, was the mistaken causal attributions (the *secondary* cognitions) brought about by the experimenters' manipulations.

PROBLEMS WITH THE THEORY

In his book *The Psychology of Affiliation*, published a few years before the Schachter–Singer study, Schachter raises some penetrating questions about his own earlier investigations. He mentions in particular a "definitional" problem:

Are we *really* talking about emotion or are we talking about opinions of emotion? Do the [emotions] of the subjects in our experiments really vary in the conforming fashion described or is it simply a verbal statement about emotion that varies? (1959:128–29)

But by the time of the Schachter and Singer study such doubts have been resolved, forgotten, or suppressed. If a subject reports that he is or feels very angry, then it is assumed that he is undergoing an emotional experience, and one that is distinct from that of fear or joy. And if by manipulating the subject's cognitions you can influence his verbal report of emotion, then it is assumed you are also influencing what he feels or experiences. Thus Schachter and Singer can claim that the self-reports indicated that subjects "had been readily manipulable into the disparate feeling states of euphoria and anger" (Schachter and Singer 1962:395).

Schachter's rationale, I imagine, is that if we are going to speak at all about what people are experiencing, we must rely on what people *say* they are experiencing, that is, the emotion labels they apply to themselves in their verbal reports. If his subjects say they are angry, then they are angry. To this "naive notion that emotion is completely defined by what a subject says," Plutchik and Ax reply, in their critique of the Schachter–Singer study, that "the whole history of clinical psychology indicates that a person's verbalization can be markedly influenced by overt or subtle suggestions" (Plutchik and Ax 1967:81).

But I think the problem goes deeper than this. Schachter is well aware that what we say in describing our emotional state is influenced by "suggestions." Indeed his *chief point* seems to be that in labeling our state we are influenced not so much by what is *felt* as by situational cues or "suggestions." In a word, emotion labeling is in his view *underdetermined* by experience. But that's precisely the problem: If Schachter is *right* about this, then what a person says in describing his emotional state must be a very poor guide to what he feels. From your report of "anger" I learn merely that you feel *aroused*. Beyond this, I learn only that there have been *external cues* that have suggested to you that you are angry. I do *not* learn that you are in a distinct *feeling-state*, namely anger. Consequently, from the disparate self-reports of the Schachter–Singer subjects we cannot infer that they had been manipulated into disparate *feeling-states*. Not, at least, if Schachter is right about the overwhelming importance of external cues in self-labeling.

It might nevertheless be asked why it should matter whether the experiment shows one's actual emotional *state* to depend on one's belief as to the cause of one's arousal, or merely shows one's self-attributions of emotion ("labeling") to depend on such a belief. One reason is that if it is only the latter, then the results support the idea that it is largely on the basis of their respective causal structures that people differentiate among the emotions, as urged in this book. But if the actual state were to remain as malleable as Schachter portrays it, then the structure of beliefs and attitudes actually causing the state would have no bearing on whether it is anger, fear, joy, or no emotional state at all. Anger would then be *not* (among other things) a state caused by a "perceived slight" but, rather, a state caused by the *belief* that one is in a state caused by a slight. This causal belief (namely, the "secondary cognition" discussed earlier in this chapter) may often happen to be *true*, but that is immaterial. All that counts is that one *believe* it true. Thus anger, like other emotions, is *arousal plus attribution*; and by experimental manipulations of such attributions, subjects had actually been manipulated into "the disparate feeling states of euphoria and anger." And where in "real life" a perceived slight causes arousal (and even, perhaps, causes a desire or impulse to harm the perpetrator), one *isn't* in fact angry at all – unless one *believes* the arousal to have been caused by the slight.

THE INFLAMMATION EXPERIMENT

This may still seem a philosopher's hairsplitting quibble. To show why I believe it is not, I have devised an experiment that parallels the Schachter and Singer experiment in important respects. First notice that, like most emotion words, the terms 'sunburn' and 'windburn' designate states that are distinguished in large part by their causes. Each designates a kind of *inflammation of the skin*: sunburn is inflammation of the skin caused by exposure to sunlight (or the ultraviolet component of sunlight), and *wind*burn is inflammation of the skin caused by irritation from exposure to wind. It is obviously important to know that human beings are *susceptible* to sunburn and to windburn. For if we know that they are susceptible to sunburn, then we know that exposure to sunlight can cause, or is apt to cause, inflammation of the skin; and similarly for windburn. If certain individuals are *more* susceptible to sunburn than others, that too is important to know. For those individuals had better be careful how much exposure to sunlight they get, if they are to avoid sunburn; and similarly for windburn.

We should expect a person who has this "common knowledge" to label inflammation of the skin (his own or another's) as "sunburn" only if he believes the condition to have been brought on by exposure to sunlight or ultraviolet light. If it has been caused solely by exposure to wind, then it isn't sunburn but windburn. And if it has been caused solely by, say, the application of some kind of *chemical* irritant, then it is neither sunburn nor windburn. (It is, one might say, a *chemical* burn.)

Here, then, is the parallel experiment. A lotion is applied to exposed skin areas of the subject. The subject is told that the lotion being applied is a vitamin supplement. Actually it contains a chemical irritant that causes a mild reddening and inflammation of the skin within an hour. Some subjects (the Informed group) are told that the vitamin supplement will probably cause some reddening of the skin, as well as some painful sensitivity to touch. Others (the Ignorant group) are not told of any side effects. Finally, the lotion applied to some subjects (the Placebo group) is an inert substance containing no irritant.

The experimenters then see to it that an alternative explanation of reddening and irritation is readily available. Some subjects are placed in a room in which they are exposed to what looks like a high-power ultraviolet sunlamp. (They are given dark goggles and told it is important that they wear them while in this room. A confederate who accompanies them remarks, "Looks to me like a sun lamp.") Other subjects are placed in a room in which a high wind has been created. A confederate remarks, "Reminds me of the day I climbed Mount Washington. Came back red as a beet!"

After an hour under these experimental conditions, once the chemical applied to their skin has taken effect, subjects are asked whether they would describe themselves as "sunburned," "windburned," or "neither." Here is my prediction. Those in the Ignorant group, who were given no idea that the lotion would cause inflammation of the skin, will be likely to check 'sunburned' or 'windburned,' depending on which room they had spent the intervening hour in. They would be unlikely to check 'neither.' On the other hand, those in the Informed group, who were told that the lotion would produce inflammation, will be significantly less likely to check 'sunburned' or 'windburned' than the Ignorant subjects. They will be more likely to check 'neither.' Finally, those to whom a nonirritating lotion was applied (the Placebo group) will also check 'neither.' For the sun lamp had actually been a weak one, not strong enough to produce noticeable inflammation of the skin; likewise, the wind to which others had been exposed was actually not strong enough or dry enough to produce noticeable inflammation. And without inflammation of the skin, they would have no reason to check either 'sunburned' or 'windburned.'

I make these predictions on the assumption that the subjects know what sunburn and windburn are, have at least a minimal capacity for drawing causal inferences, and rationally apply their knowledge and capacity to the task at hand – given the information (or misinformation) available to them. Now suppose my predictions are correct. Along comes an eminent social psychologist who says:

Gordon's results are a brilliant demonstration of my own theory of sunburn, windburn, and similar states. These states do indeed involve inflammation of the skin – indeed, inflammation of which the person is aware. But they also involve, quite obviously, a *cognitive* factor: a belief, an attribution, to the effect that one's inflammation is due to exposure to some causative agent: e.g., sunlight or wind. Sunburn is inflammation of the skin plus attribution to sunlight: more precisely, it is *the feeling state that results* (namely, that certain "sunburn feeling") when one attributes the inflammation of one's skin – *rightly or wrongly* – to sunlight. Similarly, windburn is (the feeling that results from) inflammation of the skin attributed (correctly or incorrectly) to wind.

This theory would explain why Gordon's Ignorant subjects, who attributed their chemically caused inflammation to sunlight or to wind, labeled themselves "sunburned" or "windburned," respectively; whereas his Informed subjects, who already had a perfectly good explanation of their

103

inflammation, would be less likely to report being sunburned or wind-burned. Indeed, sunburn and windburn can now be seen for what they are: *socially manipulable feeling states*, falling well within the domain of social psychology.

Not only would this be ridiculous; it would clearly trivialize the concept of "sunburn" and "windburn." The knowledge that people are susceptible to sunburn would not be knowledge about the effects of sunlight on human skin but, rather, would be knowledge about human beliefs (perhaps superstitions) about the effects of sunlight on human skin – or, if you will, the peculiar "feelings" that result from these beliefs. And the knowledge that one is *particularly* susceptible to sunburn would not give one reason to be careful about how much exposure to sunlight one gets.

I grant that the goal of predicting S's future *behavior* would be better served by asking, "What does S believe to have caused his inflammation?" (or even "Does S have the sunburn feeling?"), than by asking, "What actually caused his inflammation?" If we want to know whether S will seek relief with "sunburn salve" or with "windburn salve" (supposing that there are such distinct treatments), it will be more important to know what S believes (and "feels") than to know whether S actually has sunburn or windburn. So, too, if our purpose is to predict whether in the future S will be cautious about exposure to sunlight or cautious about exposure to wind. But these predictive aims are, of course, not what one should have in mind in seeking an account of the nature and etiology of sunburn and windburn.

Now the goal of predicting behavior is not at all irrelevant to a theory of the nature and etiology of *emotions* – which are, after all, mental or psychological states. And that, I believe, is why Schachter's interpretation of the results of his own adrenaline-arousal experiment has an air of credibility wholly absent from the above interpretation of the results of my inflammation experiment. We would expect, for example, that people who *take* themselves to be angry will *treat* themselves as angry: that they will "count to ten," consider whether the situation permits them to display their feelings openly, and so on. We might also expect a "consistency" phenomenon: People who believe themselves to be in a certain state, even if merely by inference from false premises, will tend to act *as if* they were in that state.[4] Nevertheless, for reasons that have been

4 It is relevant here to mention that the overt behavior of the Schachter–Singer

presented in earlier chapters (particularly Chapter 3), it may be important to distinguish the question 'Is S in mental state M?' from the question 'Does S think she is in M?' However, unlike the corresponding questions for sunburn, *both* of these are *psychological* questions.

In discussing James's theory of emotions I suggested that a *combined* Jamesian theory would be more plausible. Such a theory would allow that it is a person's bodily reactions to a perceived stimulus that cause him to feel the way he does when he is angry (etc.): and yet the theory would also maintain that the bodily reactions are themselves manifestations of an *underlying* state, namely *anger*. A comparable modification of *Schachter's* theory might similarly incorporate Schachter's emendation of James's view into what remains essentially the commonsense conception as I have presented it in the earlier chapters of this book. This *combined* Schachterian theory would endorse Schachter's view that it is "labeled arousal" – for instance, arousal attributed to an anger-type situation (such as a slight) – that causes a person *to feel the way he does when he is angry* (etc.). But it would also maintain that the arousal itself is a manifestation of an *underlying* state, namely *anger*. A person might in fact be in that state even though he was unaware of his arousal or ignorant of its true cause; and a person who incorrectly attributes his arousal to an anger-type situation might even *feel* (more or less) the way he does when he is angry, yet not actually be angry. A version of such a combined theory might be as represented in Figure 5.4. (I have parenthetically inserted an impulse [3] before the secondary cognition, as a highly specific manifestation of anger – a possible further departure from Schachter. There are, of course, many further ways in which this scheme might be developed.)

Of the schemes we have considered in this chapter, I think this the most promising. It depicts emotions such as anger as states quite distinct from their "labeling"; and yet it hints at a possible

subjects was found to correspond more or less closely to their self-reports. Those who, presumably because they had found themselves in an anger-provocative type of situation, reported that they felt angry tended to display more "anger behavior" in their interaction with the stooge. Likewise, those who reported themselves "happy" tended to have a high score in what the experimenters considered to be behavioral indices of euphoria. It is not clear whether this correspondence can be explained away as a consistency phenomenon. It is also not clear, however, how far a limited set of "objective" behavioral indices of emotions such as anger are to be trusted.

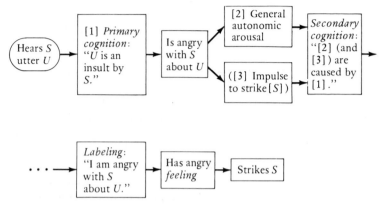

Figure 5.4.

causal role of "labeling" itself.[5] It suggests that the "recognition" of an emotion in oneself might add something of functional significance.

In concluding the discussion of Schachter's view, I want to discuss what I think is its most peculiar feature.

LABELING BY ANALOGY

Schachter's emphasis on the "labeling" of one's own mental states is best understood in the light of his important work on affiliation, hunger, and obesity, and against the background of the general theoretical framework he adopts from Festinger and other social psychologists. In that context it becomes apparent that Schachter is concerned with a certain *normative* influence on psychological self-reports. In his view, people have a need not only to define or label the state they are in but also to think of their state as "appropriate" to the circumstances, or at least as "normal" and "to be expected" in the circumstances. Under the conjoint pressure of these needs, people tend to attribute to themselves whatever they take to be the appropriate or normal state in the circumstances, whatever they think they "should" be feeling. Thus they must first determine what sort of situation they are in, and then what the

5 For a parallel suggestion, see Gordon (1984:628).

appropriate or at least normal response would be to such a situation. In order to decide what is appropriate or normal, they ordinarily turn to their own experience in similar situations in the past. But if the situation is unfamiliar or hard to define, they will try to find out how *others* are reacting to it. In this manner they decide what the appropriate or normal reaction would be. Then they attribute to themselves the same reaction.

The labeling process I have just sketched makes use of an intriguing variation of the old *argument from analogy*, long familiar in the philosophy of mind. Philosophers have used it to explain how a person can know what *another* person is feeling: Roughly, they must be feeling something like what I would be feeling if, under similar conditions, I were to behave as they do. Here, on the other hand, analogical inference is used to explain how a person decides what *he himself* is feeling: Roughly, I must be feeling something like what the behavior of others under conditions similar to mine suggests that *they* are feeling.

Such analogical reasoning may well account for some of our emotion labeling, and the extent of it is certainly a fit topic for empirical research. But notice what such reasoning presupposes. First, if people ordinarily turn to *their own* experience in similar situations in the past – if that is to be used as a basis for defining one's present state – then these past experiences, at least, must have consisted of something *more specific* than just feelings of being stirred up or aroused. If, in a situation of danger, for example, past experience in analogous situations leads me to label my present state as "fear," then my *past* reactions to danger must have been as a general rule *distinctive enough to warrant the specific label "fear."* Thus, to label one's own state by analogy to similar states in the past presupposes that as a general rule emotional reactions are identifiable without resort to analogy. In sum, analogical reasoning must be the exception, not the rule, in emotion labeling. The same must hold true when people base their judgment as to what they themselves are feeling on what *others* under similar conditions seem to be feeling. What is presupposed is that the relevant class of others (the "reference group") are themselves experiencing something more than generalized arousal.[6]

6 It would be logically consistent, I suppose, to allow a recursion: "I think I felt fear the last time I was in a situation like this. But in fact, the last time I was in

When Schachter speaks of the importance of *cognitions* concerning the eliciting situation, he apparently has in mind their role in such analogical reasoning. They enable us to make comparisons either to our own reactions in the past or to the reactions of others. But if this is what makes them important, then we should have to conclude that such cognitions are not *generally* important in emotion labeling, since analogical reasoning of the sort Schachter postulates must be the exception rather than the rule. If there is a *general* dependence of emotion labeling on causal beliefs, it must have a fundamentally different explanation. The earlier chapters of this book offer such an explanation.

Moreover, as Schachter's own work on hunger suggests, the occasional reliance on analogy or comparison is not peculiar to emotion labeling. I should guess that people are sometimes influenced, wittingly or not, by circumstantial evidence and analogy in deciding that they feel hungry, thirsty, sleepy, hot or cold, nauseous, relaxed, or sexually aroused. Indeed the labeling of any "adjectival feeling," as these have been termed by Alston, would seem liable, on occasion, to such influence.

Schachter belongs to a tradition in social psychology of seeking out the surprising revelation, especially where what is revealed is the irruption of irrationality into seemingly ordinary human affairs. What makes news, in this tradition, are phenomena that systematically run counter to expectations of "naive" or commonsense psychology. Schachter himself has pioneered in demonstrating experimentally the surprising influence of external cues, analogical inference, and suggestion on the labeling of such "felt" or "experienced" states as hunger, thirst, and pain.

When it comes to emotions, Schachter holds such influence to be the tail that wags the dog. They are, together with arousal, *the* basis of emotion labeling, as well as, indeed, the source of emotion. As I have argued, this cannot be correct. Yet I think it no accident that it is in his treatment of emotions, in particular, that Schachter has inflated his account of social-psychological influences into a full-blown theory. Such inflation would have been unthinkable in the

such a situation, I had determined I was feeling fear from observation of my friend, who behaved as if he was feeling fear. And he, in turn, behaved that way because he thought he was feeling fear; and he thought this chiefly because in a similar situation in *his* past he had felt fear." And so on. Limited empirical inquiry suggests that a *universal* recursion of this sort is not to be found.

case of hunger or pain, for example. It would have been patently absurd to theorize that no one labels his state "hunger" unless he believes himself to be in a "hunger-type situation," such as one in which several hours have elapsed since he last ate; or that no one labels his state "pain" unless he attributes it to an appropriate stimulus. Only in the case of emotions do such generalizations seem at all apt. The reason, however, is not that human beings happen to be especially suggestible when it comes to the labeling of emotions. The reason concerns rather the nature of emotion concepts: the fact that the very definitions of most of our emotion terms include causal stipulations. The relationship between emotion labeling and cognition may be surprising, but its explanation seems to require no psychological theory beyond that embodied in commonsense psychology.

6

The passivity of emotions

A number of philosophers object to the traditional classification of fear, joy, jealousy, embarrassment, and the like – collectively, "the emotions" – as "passions": ways, or products of ways, of "being acted on." For it is thought that if the emotions are passions, a proper attitude toward them would be one of helplessness and fatalistic resignation. If the emotions are passions, then, according to some, we are not responsible for them. Edward Sankowski expresses the view succinctly:

> We are often tempted to think of emotions in general as phenomena which are not under the control of those who feel them, as "passions" with respect to which we are passive, as phenomena which happen to us rather than as phenomena we may bring into being somehow. Adequate understanding of the relations between action and emotion, however, shows this to be bad faith. (1977:834–35)

Some writers have even thought it necessary, in combating such *mauvaise foi*, not only to deny that these states are passions but even to assert that they are to be classified among our *actions*. Robert C. Solomon sums up his view as follows: "Emotions are judgments and actions, not occurrences or happenings that we suffer. Accordingly, I want to say that emotions are choices and our responsibility" (1973: 40). Evidently Solomon thinks that to conceive emotions as passions is to conceive them as *involuntary* states. The remedy he proposes is that they be conceived instead as actions.

I think the attack on the passivity of emotions trades on a common misconception of what the passivity consists in: of what it is for something to be a passion. Contrary to the assumption of a number of philosophers, it is not a consequence of the passivity of emotions that they are states with respect to which *we* are passive. More specifically, neither of the following is a consequence:

- That emotions are *states that act on us*
- That emotions are *involuntary states*, states that are not "up to us"

(To show this will be the burden of a later section, "Two Fallacies".)

The main *positive* thesis I put forward in this chapter is presented in the final section, "The Causal Structure of a Passion." There I point to a certain difference between emotions and actions and argue that it is this difference that underlies the traditional and intuitive classification of emotions as "passions," or ways (or products of ways) of being acted upon. Let me anticipate by giving the general outlines of that thesis.

What emotions *share* with actions is, most importantly, an origin in propositional attitudes rather than in "brute" causes exclusively. If, for example, the sight of some particular person causes fear, anger, embarrassment, or joy, it does so, at least typically, by way of one's *beliefs and attitudes* concerning that person. But not everything that is caused by beliefs and attitudes is an intentional action, of course: It all depends (or at least mostly depends) on *how the beliefs and attitudes interlock*. Where intentional action, or at least *rational* intentional action, is concerned, we often find the following pattern: a positive or a negative attitude toward some possible state of affairs S – such as a "wish" or a "desire" for S – engaging with an *instrumental* or *means-end* belief, one that functions as *an instruction for bringing about* (or avoiding) S. (There are alternative patterns as well.)

But beliefs and pro-con attitudes sometimes interlock in a distinctly different way, as we have seen in earlier chapters. Notoriously, a wish for S may meet up with the "cold, hard fact" – or, at least, the cold, hard *belief* (be it true or false) – that S *cannot be*. Such *wish-frustrations* (as I have termed such engagements of pro-con attitude with belief) has certain characteristic *effects* on human beings. Stated baldly and boldly (not to mention vaguely), my view has been that we use words such as 'displeased,' 'sad,' and 'upset' to baptize some of these effects, and more specialized emotion terms such as 'angry,' 'indignant,' 'embarrassed,' and 'ashamed' to mark the effects of particular *types* of wish-frustration, for instance the *knowing and willful* frustration of one's wish by someone else. In addition to words that designate "negative factive emotions" (as I call this most populous class of emotions) there are others, such as 'pleased,' 'proud,' 'afraid,' and 'hopeful,' that signalize effects of *still other* patterns of engagement between cognitive and pro-con types of propositional attitudes.

111

It will, of course, be crucial to ask *why* a difference in such patterns of engagement, or "causal structures," is relevant to the distinction between "actions" and "passions": why propositional attitudes that interlock in one way give rise to effects we view as "actions," whereas effects of other patterns of propositional attitudes are viewed as "passions."

I begin the argument of this chapter with a datum on which consensus is easily attained: the *grammatical* passivity of emotion descriptions.

PASSIONS AND PARTICIPLES

Grammatical evidence suggests that the "passivity" of states such as fear, anger, and jealousy is not an invention of philosophers or psychologists. That the so-called emotions belong to the category of "passions," or states produced by one's being *acted on* in certain ways, is suggested by the fact that the great majority of adjectives designating emotions are derived from participles: for example, 'amused,' 'annoyed,' 'astonished,' 'delighted,' 'depressed,' 'embarrassed,' 'frightened,' 'horrified,' 'irritated,' 'miffed,' 'overjoyed,' 'pleased,' 'terrified,' 'surprised,' 'troubled,' 'upset,' and 'vexed.' Some others, such as 'afraid' and 'sad,' can only claim participial ancestors: for instance, 'afraid' was originally a participle of the verb 'affray,' and 'sad' descends from the etymological forbear of 'sated.'[1] There are current colloquial and slang emotion descriptions that suggest that the participial model remains a compelling one: 'tickled,' 'ticked off,' 'burned up,' 'juiced up,' 'bent out of shape,' and so on.

It might, of course, be true that the alleged passivity of emotions remains an invention, after all – an invention of a metaphysics that is naively based on a purely grammatical "decision" (albeit one common to all or most human languages) to generate adjectives of emotion from verbs. Still another possibility is this: The emotions are indeed "passive" in some important (perhaps metaphysical)

---

1 In addition, 'angry' originally meant (according to the *Oxford English Dictionary*) 'troublesome' or 'vexatious,' as in 'that which *troubles*' or 'that which *vexes*,' and later came to designate the corresponding *effect*: being troubled or vexed. (In modern use, the term is more specific.) On the other hand, 'sorry,' and 'enjoy' appear to bear no historical traces of transitivity. Hence I refer only to the 'great majority' of emotion adjectives.

112

sense, but the grammatical passivity of emotion adjectives arose independently, not as a reflection of passivity in that deeper sense.

Bearing these possibilities in mind, I think it is important, as a prelude to any further discussion of the passivity of emotions, to get clear about the type of passivity that is at least *suggested* by the grammatical passivity of emotion adjectives. For this purpose it will pay to compare adjectives that designate emotional states with *other* adjectives that are derived from participles. Perhaps more important, this exercise will show us what types of passivity are *not* (or should not be) suggested by the grammatical passivity of emotion adjectives.

The emotion words mentioned above belong to a class of adjectives that includes 'magnetized,' 'frozen,' 'rotten,' 'hardened,' 'torn,' 'salted,' 'pickled,' 'congealed,' 'solidified,' 'intoxicated,' 'irritated' (as a condition, e.g., of the skin), and 'exposed' (as a state, e.g., of photographic film). Such adjectives describe something's *state or condition* in terms of the particular type of *operation* or *change of state* that induces it. Thus, to ask whether the apple is rotten is to ask whether it is in the condition that is (at least typically) brought about in apples by rotting; to ask whether the film is exposed is to ask whether it is in the state that is at least typically brought about in film by exposing it to light. The qualification "at least typically" is needed to cover, for instance, a variety of apples that have been genetically engineered to be physically and chemically indistinguishable from rotten apples; and films that have been manufactured to be physically and chemically indistinguishable from film that has been exposed to light. Such apples may be said to be "rotten" apples, although they have never undergone rotting; such films, to be "exposed" films, although they have never undergone exposure to light.

Within this class, a further division may be made. For something may freeze, rot, congeal, or solidify (changes of state designated by intransitive verbs) without the intervention of an "agent" (or, perhaps, catalyst) that freezes, rots, congeals, or solidifies it (transitive verb). A food is salted or pickled, on the other hand, only if it has been salted or pickled, typically by a person using the appropriate substance (salt, a pickling solution, etc.): It doesn't just "salt" or "pickle." Likewise, a person is *intoxicated* only if something (an intoxic*ant*) is, or at least has been, intoxicating him. One does not simply "intoxicate." *Intoxicated* is an adjective that char-

113

acterizes a state as resulting from an *operation* performed by some "agent."

Emotion terms belong to the latter, "transitive" class. A person does not simply amuse, annoy, astonish, delight, depress, embarrass, frighten, horrify, overjoy, terrify, or surprise: These too are *not* changes of state designated by intransitive verbs.[2] For X to be, for instance, embarrassed, is for X to be in a state that is produced by *something's (or someone's) embarrassing X*. In this respect,

> Mary is embarrassed.

is comparable to any of the following:

> The film is exposed.
>
> The iron bar is magnetized.
>
> The shirt is torn.
>
> Mary is intoxicated.

We should note that it is also comparable to any of the following:

> Mary is convinced that _____.
>
> Mary is persuaded that _____.
>
> Mary is resolved that _____.[3]

The adjectives 'convinced' and 'persuaded' seem to pose a bit of a problem. For, even though one does not simply "convince" or "persuade" (intransitive), it is not clear that a person is convinced (that something is so) only if something (e.g., a reason, or a reasoner) *convinces*, or *has convinced*, him. For 'is convinced that _____' would seem at least loosely interchangeable with 'is fairly certain that _____.' Nevertheless, 'is convinced' describes one's state or condition in terms of a type of operation that *typically* induces it. To be convinced (of something), we may say, is to be in a state that is at least *typically* brought on by someone's or something's convincing one (of something). We might compare these adjectives to what is sometimes classified as an emotion term: 'depressed.' A person doesn't just "depress"; yet it would appear that a person may just *become depressed* – that is, without being depressed *by*

---

2 I leave aside the special construction 'He surprises easily.'

3 These examples were brought to my attention by an anonymous reader for *The Philosophical Review*, in which this chapter originally appeared (in a slightly different version). There are some grammatical differences, it might be noted. Consider the following form of speech: 'It embarrasses (or: terrifies, upsets) me that *p*,' which may be paraphrased, '(The fact) That *p* embarrasses (or: terrifies, upsets) me.' Notice that we do not have the parallel formulation, 'It convinces (or: persuades, resolves) me that *p*,' to be paraphrased, 'The fact that *p* convinces (or: persuades, resolves) me.'

114

anything. Again, to describe someone as "depressed" is to describe him as in a state of a type at least typically brought on by someone's or something's depressing someone.

Some of the participial adjectives I have mentioned characterize a state as the effect of a specific type of *"brute" noncognitive* cause. To speak of someone as "intoxicated," for example, is to characterize his state as caused by the intake of alcohol (etc.), not in terms of any *beliefs* or *attitudes* that may enter into its causal history. A brute-cause state such as intoxication may strike us a paradigm of a "passive" state. It may be enlightening, therefore, to notice what the "passivity" of *even* a brute-cause state such as intoxication is compatible with: particularly, the degree of control, freedom, and responsibility it allows.

First, although one does not simply "intoxicate," this is not to say that one could not *cause oneself to be intoxicated.* This is something one does by way of doing something else, namely, administering (or causing someone to administer) an intoxicant. One can also prevent oneself from being intoxicated. This may be done by preventing the administration of an intoxicant; or possibly, even *after intake* of an intoxicant, by taking measures that prevent it from "taking effect." For intoxication may depend on, among other things, the presence (or the absence) of certain *other* substances besides the intoxicant itself; thus one may be able to take, for instance, the appropriate "antagonist" or "antidote." A training regimen may also affect some of the conditions on which intoxication depends. Finally, even where the intoxicant has already *taken effect,* one may be able to curb some of the effects of intoxication, particularly effects on overt behavior.

What is far more interesting, however, is the possibility that *at moderate dosage levels* certain substances (e.g., psychoactive drugs such as alcohol or marijuana) will intoxicate a person only if he *wants* them to intoxicate him, or only if he actively "assents" in some way to the intoxication. Or it may be that with some substances, some subjects, and some dosage levels, a subject becomes intoxicated only if he first *believes* he is (or will become) intoxicated. If, indeed, such "attitudinal" or "cognitive" factors enter in, we might have an explanation of the apparent effects of suggestion and social *milieu* on degree of intoxication.

Were these points to carry over to emotions such as embarrassment, we should say the following: One does not simply *embarrass* (intransitive verb): rather, there must be something that embarrasses one. (We commonly call a source of embarrassment "an embarrassment," but since this term is ambiguous, I shall maintain the analogy with intoxication by speaking of "an embarrass*ant*.") But this "passivity," once again, does not preclude *causing oneself to be* embarrassed. This would be done by way of doing something else, namely, seeing to it that there is an embarrassant. One can also prevent oneself from being embarrassed. This may be done by preventing the existence of an embarrassant; or possibly, even despite the existence of an embarrassant, by taking measures that prevent it from "taking effect." Embarrassment, or at least one particular person's embarrassment on one particular occasion, may happen to depend on the availability or unavailability of certain chemicals at particular receptor sites in the brain. Thus, intake of the right drug may have the effect of ridding the subject of his embarrassment altogether. Similarly, a training regimen may also affect some of the conditions on which such a state depends. Finally, even where the embarrassant has already *taken effect*, one may be able to curb some of the effects of embarrassment, particularly effects on behavior.

But as with intoxication, what is particularly interesting is the possibility that the embarrassant, at least for some subjects under some conditions, will embarrass only if the subject *wants* it to, or only if he actively "assents" in some way to being embarrassed by it. Again, it may be that a subject actually becomes embarrassed only if he first *believes* he is (or will become) embarrassed. If such "attitudinal" or "cognitive" factors do enter in, we might have an explanation of the apparent effects of suggestion and social *milieu*.[4] Indeed, if the frequency and severity of "physical" pain depends to a significant degree on cultural variables, as some studies indicate, it should not be surprising that the felt "awfulness" of the object or content of embarrassment, envy, or jealousy might also depend on such variables.

I have been assuming thus far a perfect analogy between being intoxicated and being embarrassed. Their belonging to a common grammatical category does not assure us of this, of course. And there surely are some important disanalogies. For one thing, *em-*

---

4 This is, of course, not to endorse Schachter's theory, which takes the actual identity of a person's emotion to be a function, in part, of social suggestion.

barrassants are not ingested substances but perceived (or otherwise "cognized") states of affairs, and the effects of such cognitions notoriously depend on what *other* cognitive and attitudinal states a person is in. My suggestion, therefore, is *not* that the answers to such questions are just the same for embarrassment and other emotions as those for being intoxicated. The comparison is useful, I think, only in showing that the *grammatically* passive character of *being intoxicated* is compatible with the subject's having *a wide range of active roles* to play in controlling his state. Any of the points of possible intervention I have mentioned should be taken into consideration, it would seem, in an adequate treatment of *responsibility* for being intoxicated or for being embarrassed. Attributions of responsibility may depend on the particulars of the situation in ways far more complex than most discussions have indicated.

TWO FALLACIES

That emotions are ways, or products of ways, of being acted on warrants the conclusion that we are passive with respect to (i.e., acted on by) something. But it does not tell us *what* acts on us, what the "agent" is. It plainly does not imply that the agent is the emotion: the fear, the embarrassment, or whatever.

It is common to assume otherwise. Consider the following appositions from the passage quoted at the beginning of this chapter:

- "passions" with respect to which we are passive
- phenomena which are not under the control of those who feel them
- phenomena which happen to us rather than . . . phenomena we may bring into being somehow. (Sankowski 1977:834–35)

The first of these implies that if emotions are passions, then we are passive *with respect to them.* But '*x* is passive with respect to *y*' *seems* to entail '*y* is active with respect to *x*,' which is naturally understood to mean '*y* acts on *x*.' Perhaps we may gloss 'passive with respect to' differently. But in any case, it is important to note that *y* may be a way, or a product of a way, in which *x* is acted on, even though all of the following are true:

> *y* does not act on *x*;
>
> *y* is under the control of *x*;
>
> *y* does not just "happen" to *x* but is on the contrary invariably brought on by *x*.

117

It must be said that some philosophers who have *defended* the thesis that the emotions are ways of being acted upon have been prone to draw the unhappy conclusion that we are victims of our own emotions. R. S. Peters, for one, quite rightly insists that the emotions are not simply judgments or "appraisals" of an object or situation, as E. Bedford's "Emotions" had suggested (Bedford 1956–7; Peters 1961–2). For such a sanitized view overlooks the fact that a judgment or appraisal may be "the reason for or the cause of our being *affected* or *acted on*"; and only then would our state be described as an "emotion." So far, so good. But Peters implies that when we are thus acted upon, it is *our emotion* that acts on us. Not only do emotions, "like the weather, come over us"; sometimes they even "overcome" us. Therein, Peters believes, lies the *passivity* that Bedford's appraisal theory overlooks. The passivity of emotions is a matter "of judgments being disturbed, clouded, or warped by emotion, of people not being properly in control of their emotions, being subject to gusts of emotion" (1961–2:119).

Here Peters has made a wrong turn. Whether or not it is true that emotions often seem to come over a person like a change of weather, whether or not emotions sometimes seem to toss us about like ships in a storm, and so on, none of this is a consequence of the supposition that emotions are passions or ways of being acted on. The same error underlies the protest of other writers that fear, embarrassment, and the like must *not* be regarded as passions, lest we see ourselves as their helpless and blameless victims. It is an error worth setting right.

To say that emotions are types of states in which *something* acts on us is not to say that *emotions* act on us – much less, that they are liable to *overcome* us. Embarrassment (to take a representative example) is a way of being acted upon, in that, if we are embarrassed, then *something embarrasses us*: typically, some (putative) *state of affairs*, such as our having revealed to the audience our unpreparedness, or our being asked a question that threatens to reveal our unpreparedness. But it is one thing to say that some *state of affairs S* acts on us, and quite another to say that *our being embarrassed (by S)* acts on us. It is a fallacy to infer, from the assumption that the term "embarrassment" characterizes a person's state as a product of something's having acted on him, that *the resulting state* – embarrassment – also acts on (much less "comes over" or "overcomes") the person. It is similarly fallacious to infer that a *second*

118

state of affairs, namely that of his *being embarrassed* by S, also acts on or comes over him. One cannot properly draw the conclusion

> x is a state that acts on (a person),

from either of the following:

> x is a state of being acted on in a certain way
>
> x is a state produced by being acted on in a certain way.

There is a second type of fallacy that clouds the issue of the passivity of emotions. It involves the unwarranted inference from

> x is a state of (or: produced by) being acted on in a certain way

to

> x is an *involuntary* state.

Such an inference, as I have noted, seems to underlie Solomon's assumption that the only way to avoid regarding emotions as involuntary is to suppose that they are not passions but actions.

We can see from the comparison with intoxication that this is a faulty inference: although *intoxicated* is an adjective that characterizes a state as resulting from an *operation* performed by some "agent," such a characterization rules out none of the following:

- That a person may *cause himself to be* intoxicated
- That a person may prevent himself from being intoxicated, by preventing the administration of an intoxicant; by taking measures that prevent an intoxicant, once present, from "taking effect"; or perhaps simply by refusing to "assent" to being intoxicated

The passivity of embarrassment, similarly, rules out none of these options. To dramatize the point, imagine all human beings to have come into the world equipped with a toggle switch that made embarrassment *wholly optional*. Only when the switch is in the "on" position can any state of affairs embarrass a person. Imagine also a backup button with the function of "erasing" any embarrassment that may be caused when the toggle is "on." Imagine even a second backup button with the function of causing any unerased embarrassment to sit idle until the button is pushed a second time: leaving, in the meanwhile, not even a disposition to the feelings and behavior typical of embarrassment, but a second-order disposition – to have such a disposition when the button is pressed again. For human beings thus equipped, embarrassment would be at least doubly optional, its manifestations triply so. Yet embarrassment would remain, for them as for us, a way of being acted on, a passion.

119

These people, when they are embarrassed, are embarrassed by something.

Let me propose another image: A new race of human beings comes into the world with all of these controls *internalized*. *Desire* toggles on or off the possibility of embarrassment: When you *want* embarrassing situations to embarrass, they may do so; when you do not want them to, they won't. Similarly for the "erase" button: The onset of a desire not to have the embarrassment one presently is disposed to feel and act from erases the present embarrassment. And so on. Still, when these people are embarrassed, they are embarrassed, acted on, by something. In short, the grammatically passive character of 'embarrassed' – the fact that it is an adjective that characterizes a state as resulting from an operation performed by some "agent" – is compatible with the subject's having a wide range of active roles to play in controlling his state.

The question of control over emotions must be distinguished from another: that of control over the states of affairs that are the "agents" of our emotions. In Chapter 4 I put forward the suggestion that most if not all of the states commonly classified as "emotions" are about states of affairs not presently under the subject's control. Not only are we acted on by something; we are acted on by something over which we have, at the time, no control. For example, there is nothing Mary may do now to prevent the publicity that she is embarrassed by (or about) – for it is publicity that has already occurred. It may indeed be true that an embarrassing state of affairs *S*, being in general a fait accompli, properly evokes an attitude of helplessness, of being unable to bring it about presently *that S does not obtain*. Even our fears, though they concern matters that are uncertain, appear to be restricted to uncertainties that are not matters to be resolved by our own decision or fiat: roughly, to awful possibilities that are beyond our control. None of this entails, however, that we are similarly helpless with regard to whether some state of affairs over which we have no control *embarrasses* us, or whether some awful possibility that is beyond our control shall be *feared true*. Although in emotions generally we are acted on by something over which we have, at the time, no control, we may very well have control over whether we are thus acted on.

Let me run quickly over the ground we have covered thus far. States such as embarrassment are states characterized as resulting from an *operation* performed by some "agent." In general the

120

"agent" is identical with the state of affairs one is embarrassed about. (Matters are more complicated where the "forward-looking" emotions are concerned.) Although I find it useless to generalize about "the emotions," it appears that most of the states commonly so designated are states characterized in this way. But to characterize a state as resulting from an operation performed by some "agent" is not to characterize it as a *state with respect to which we are passive*: neither as a *state that acts on us* nor as an *involuntary state*, a state that is not "up to us."

THE CAUSAL STRUCTURE OF A PASSION

Given the similarities between the causal components of emotions and those of actions, why are emotions categorized, in our grammar and in our common thought, as passions? Putting the point more perspicuously, why do we characterize certain states as products of a person's being acted on by a state of affairs S, rather than as an action performed by the person because of S, such as where S, or the fact that S obtains, is characterized as *a reason for which the person acted*? For example, why do we not say that the publicizing of the wedding was *Mary's reason for "embarrassing"*?

I am not concerned to show that there is *no* sense of the term 'action' in which emotions are classifiable as "actions." It is true that actions are (or at least, essentially involve) a species of *events*, whereas emotions are *states*. But if we focus on *changes* of state or *onsets* of states (*becoming* angry, embarrassed, grateful, etc.), we can say that these are indeed actions in some very broad sense: To grow angry is to "do something," in the sense in which a melon does something when it grows ripe, a cloud does something when it changes shape, or a lock does something when it opens. My concern, however, is not with just any sense of "acting" or "doing something" but with a sense that bears on the issues of *control* and *responsibility* that were of concern to the authors cited at the beginning of this chapter. Although I have argued that for something *x* to be a *passion* I undergo does not require that *x* be outside my control or my domain of responsibility, neither does it require that *x* be *within* my control or my domain of responsibility. On the other hand, for something *x* to be an action that I have performed intentionally or for a reason *does* seem to carry a *presumption* that *x* was at least to some degree within my control and that I am at

121

least to some degree responsible for having done it. The question to be addressed is, Why are emotions, given their dependence on our desires or attitudes as well as on our beliefs, not actions in *this* sense?

My answer is that although emotions and actions are each causally dependent on both cognitive and attitudinal states, there is a systematic difference in the *contents* of these states and the *logical relationships* that obtain among them when they produce emotional states, as distinct from intentional behavior. Very roughly, the difference is that when one *acts for a reason*, one's action is caused by attitudes and beliefs that are related in the following way: *Given* the attitude, what is believed (the content of the belief) "says something in favor of," or "argues for" so acting.[5] On the other hand, the attitudes and beliefs that underlie, say, embarrassment, are not so related: It is not true that given the attitude, what is believed "says something in favor of," "argues for" *being embarrassed*. For the underlying attitudes and beliefs concern the "object" or "content" of the embarrassment, that is, what one is embarrassed about – not the state of being embarrassed. Corresponding to this difference is a difference in the *forms of argument* appropriate to talking a person out of (or into) actions and emotions, respectively. I shall take up these points in order: first, the difference between the causal structures of emotions and rational actions; then, the difference in forms of argument.

As I argue in Chapters 2 through 4, the negative and positive emotions are caused, respectively, by a negative or a positive *attitude* toward something that is (believed to be) the case, or toward some epistemic possibility – something that might (for all one knows) be the case. Thus, if Mary is embarrassed by the publicity about her wedding, then among the "sustaining causes" of her embarrassment is her wishing there not to be such publicity and her believing that there is or has been such publicity.

Contrast this with acting for a reason. Suppose that Mary actually undertakes certain measures to gain or to avoid publicity about her wedding: She decides to get married in Mexico, say. In that case, among the causes of her behavior would be, as with the emotions, a positive or a negative attitude toward there being publicity about it, such as a wish or a desire that there (not) be such publicity. But

5 Leaving aside cases where one's action is not as one had intended.

in a fully explicit statement of Mary's reason for acting, this attitude would be *connected* with some type of behavior, for instance, her having the wedding in Mexico. A *cognitive* state, typically, would provide the bridge. Instead of a belief that there is, has been, or might be publicity, the relevant belief would be (typically) an *instrumental* or *means-end* belief, namely, that *by* acting this way – by holding the wedding in Mexico – one will or at least might gain (avoid) publicity. This belief functions as an instruction for gaining, or at least possibly helping to gain, the *satisfaction* of the wish or desire. There are other ways in which beliefs may rationally "connect up" attitudes and behavior. For example, I may have a desire to act a certain way if (or when) a certain condition is satisfied, for instance, if someone has done me a great favor, or when someone has violated a regulation I am entrusted to enforce. In such cases the belief serves not to tell me what type of action to perform but *whether* (or *when*) and *to whom* I am to perform a stipulated type of action.

In any case, actions performed for a reason are not only *caused* by our attitudes and beliefs. They are, in a sense, *prescribed, dictated,* or at least *justified* by the attitudes and beliefs that cause them.[6] For example: Given a negative attitude toward the wedding's being publicized, the premise that having the wedding in Mexico will make publicity less likely *says something in favor of* having the wedding in Mexico. Given a favorable attitude toward reciprocating favors, the premise that Henry has done me a favor would be *an argument for* my doing Henry a favor. In general, *given* the pro-con attitude underlying the action, *what* is believed (the "content" of the belief) *counts in favor of* so acting.

Given the supposition that pro-con attitudes can be verbalized (verbally expressed) as value judgments – judgments of "desirability" – my point is essentially the same as one made several years ago by Davidson:

Corresponding to the belief and attitude of a primary reason for an action, we can always construct (with a little ingenuity) the premises of a syllogism from which it follows that the action has some (as Anscombe calls it) "desirability characteristic." (1963:690)

The logical relationship between the beliefs and attitudes that enter into the analyses of the various *emotions*, on the other hand,

6 More specifically, by those that constitute the reason with which one acts.

123

is quite different. Mary's negative attitude toward publicity – her wish that the wedding not be publicized – and her belief that the wedding *has been publicized* do not cause embarrassment by "saying something in favor of" being embarrassed. Her embarrassment was not "dictated" or "called for" by this belief together with her attitude toward publicity. She might, of course, have an additional belief that embarrassment *would* produce a certain beneficial result, for example, evoke such sympathy that the publicity she is embarrassed about *will not continue*. And that belief might affect the *side conditions* in a way that makes it more probable that she will be embarrassed. Conceivably – in some individuals, at least – such an instrumental belief is *causally necessary* for emotions of a given type. But the belief that enters into the *analysis* of her embarrassment – the belief *in virtue of which* she is embarrassed by or about the publicity, that is, embarrassed *that the wedding received publicity* – is not a belief that her embarrassment will or might somehow do some good, much less a belief that it will, specifically, *undo* the state of affairs she is embarrassed about. It is the same with *gratitude*: One may have a favorable attitude toward feeling gratitude for great favors. But the attitude that enters into the *analysis* of gratitude – the attitude in virtue of which I can be said to be *grateful* for what Henry did – is an attitude *toward what Henry did*, not an attitude toward my being grateful for what Henry did.

I turn now to the forms of criticism and argument to which actions and emotions are sensitive. Because they are causally dependent on one's desires, wishes, normative beliefs, and attitudes, human emotions are, like actions performed for a reason, typically responsive to *verbal reasoning* of the right sort. By "reasoning with" a person one may be able to talk him into regretting something, or being embarrassed by something, or being angry about something. Similarly, one may be able to talk someone out of such states.

There is, however, a crucial difference in the *forms of argument* used to talk a person into (or out of) actions and emotions, respectively. In the case of *actions* a fully explicit reason (e.g., the premises of a practical syllogism) entails, as suggested, a positive evaluation of *the action itself* (under some description). For example, the premises

1. It would be awful if the wedding received publicity.

and

2. *Getting married in Mexico* would prevent the wedding from receiving publicity.

entail

> *Getting married in Mexico* would prevent something awful from happening.[7]

Where emotions are concerned, the relevant verbal reasoning has a different logical structure. I said earlier that if Mary is embarrassed by the publicity about her wedding, then what is keeping her that way is (among other things) a negative attitude toward there being publicity about it and a belief that there is or has been such publicity. The relevant "premises" would be as follows. Corresponding to (and expressing) the requisite negative attitude would be a negative normative or evaluative premise such as the one given for action:

1. It would be awful if the wedding received publicity.

But corresponding to the belief we would have, in place of (2), the premise,

3. The wedding has received publicity.

If Mary is *glad* that there is publicity, the second premise would remain the same, but the first premise (1) would be replaced by a positive evaluation; for instance:

4. It would be lovely if the wedding received publicity.

If she *fears* there will be publicity, then the first premise would be (1) once again, but the second premise would be one that expressed lack of certainty that there will not be publicity; for example:

5. The wedding may (for all I know) have received publicity.

Here, then, is the crucial difference. Whereas a fully explicit reason for an *action* entails a positive evaluation of *the action itself*, for example, getting married in Mexico, a reason for an emotion such as gladness, embarrassment, or fear does *not* entail a positive (or negative) evaluation of *the emotion itself*, for example, the gladness, the embarrassment, or the fear. Instead, as noted earlier, it

---

7 The positive evaluation of actions that prevent what is awful may be made explicit, if necessary.

entails an evaluation of the "object" or "content" of the emotion.[8] *In virtue of its causal structure alone*, we can expect intentional actions to be responsive to reasoning concerning the goodness or badness of so acting. This does not hold for emotions. It cannot be said *in virtue of its causal structure alone*, that embarrassment will respond to reasoning concerning the goodness or badness of being embarrassed. Instead, we can expect embarrassment to be responsive to reasoning concerning the "object" or "content" of the embarrassment: where someone is embarrassed "about a certain state of affairs *S*," reasoning as to whether *S* actually obtains, and reasoning as to whether *S* is bad.[9]

Once again, it should be emphasized that the causal components in virtue of which someone's state counts as embarrassment, or more specifically as embarrassment about the wedding's getting publicity, only make a person "ripe" for sustaining a particular emotion. The right side-conditions must obtain as well. That offers a possible point of entry for *voluntary control*, as I suggested earlier in this chapter. Our attitudes toward being in particular states, such as embarrassment or embarrassment about a given matter, may very well affect side conditions without which the emotion would not occur. Criticism of such states may have an effect on the frequency with which they arise.[10]

What emerges is that intentional actions and emotions are each produced by systems that are responsive to our desires and (at least typically) capable of "listening to reason," particularly to argu-

---

8 If a positive emotion such as gladness were about *itself* – were its own object or content – then, I submit, it might be indistinguishable from an intentional action: The agent would intentionally gladden. But this seems never to be so. One may, I suppose, be glad *that one is glad* about something specific, or glad that one is just *glad* (about something or other). But there is a distinction here between first- and second-order gladness, the gladness one is glad about and the gladness about it. The *second-order* gladness may be responsive to arguments regarding the goodness of the *first-order gladness*. But it does not hinge on arguments regarding the goodness of this second-order gladness itself. (And similarly for gladness of higher orders.)

9 This is a simplification. Embarrassment has further cognitive and attitudinal complications, hence is sensitive to reasoning about additional "topics."

10 In addition, of course, a negative evaluation of an emotion of some type such as embarrassment, anger, envy, or jealousy can at least have a dissuasive effect on *actions* motivated by these emotions. For example, where anger causes a desire to harm the person one is angry with, which in turn would cause one to do something to harm that individual, a negative evaluation either of anger in general or of one's particular anger may damp the *expression* of this desire.

126

ments, and refutations of arguments, that apply norms, standards, or values. But they respond to arguments of significantly different forms. And this difference in form accounts for our intuition that *in virtue of* intentionally Xing we are, in general, responsible agents, answerable to norms concerning Xing; whereas we are not answerable to norms concerning being embarrassed, angry, or jealous merely in virtue of being embarrassed, angry, or jealous.

This is a subtle difference that becomes apparent only upon comparative analysis of the causal structures of actions and passions. Yet it should be fundamental to any discussion of "responsibility for emotions."

7

Folk psychology, pretend play, and the normality of knowledge

Implicit in much of this book is an assumption that our commonsense theory of emotions is embedded in a larger conceptual framework: what is often referred to as "commonsense" or "folk" psychology. That framework embraces, among others, the concepts of belief, wish, and desire, which I have invoked to explain the differences between

· Factive and epistemic emotions
· Negative and positive emotions
· One specific emotion type (e.g., anger) and another (e.g., indignation)
· States of the same emotion type with different sententially specified "contents": for example, anger about Junior's having ruined the pictures, anger about having to go to work at 6:00 A.M.
· Emotions and actions

In this final chapter, I present a brief account of the nature of that larger conceptual framework. Although one can provide quite a bit of systematic insight into the so-called emotions without delving into the broader issues, I have a special reason to discuss the nature of folk psychology and, indeed, to do so in a new way. I want to give an account that will explain the prevalence of *factivity* in our emotion concepts. To do this is of added interest because factivity also pervades the scheme of explanation that is widely thought to be the very core of folk psychology: *rational explanation*, in which one explains S's action in terms of the *reasons for which S* acts (Unger 1975).

THE NORMALITY OF KNOWLEDGE

In Chapters 2 and 3 it was argued that a strong *epistemic* attribution – of *knowledge*, as opposed to mere *belief* – is implicit in standard attributions of factive emotions. That is, in such contexts as 'Smith regrets _____,' 'Smith is upset _____,' and 'Smith is delighted _____,' sentential complements become factive, implying both truth and knowledge – indeed, ineluctably so, even after the prepositions 'about' or 'of' (e.g., 'proud of _____').[1] To avoid factivity one resorts to a causal circumlocution, assigning sentential content only to a *belief*:

Smith is upset because he believes (thinks) _____.

The cause (source) of Smith's upset is his belief that _____.

It is striking that all standard attributions of emotions that imply *belief* carry the stronger epistemic implication of *knowledge*. Standard attributions of *reasons* (for action, emotion, belief, or desire) also imply not mere belief but knowledge, if the following thesis of Unger's is right: "If *S*'s reason (for something *X*) *is that p*, then *S knows* that *p*" (1975:200). Whether or not Unger is right about reasons in general, it does appear that if *S X*'s *because p*, where the term 'because' is understood to introduce a statement of a *reason of S*'s, then *S* knows that *p*. 'Because' contexts are always factive or truth-entailing. And if '*p*' is understood to state a reason of *S*'s, then *S* believes that *p*. Finally, the best explanation of the true belief condition appears to be that it is symptomatic of a still stronger condition: *knowledge* that *p*.

Why then is so strong an epistemic implication *standard*? It was noted in Chapter 3 that on a causal or a reliability account of factual knowledge, the Knowledge Condition has the consequence that if Smith is upset or delighted (about the fact) that Dewey won, then Smith's upset (delight) is causally or at least counterfactually linked to *Dewey's having won*. (This explains why one finds it natural to replace 'about the fact that' with 'because' and to equate what Smith is upset or delighted about with the "cause" or "source" of Smith's upset or delight. As noted in Chapter 6, most of the terms for emotions carry their causality on their face: They are adjectives derived from participles, designating *passions*, or states produced by one's being acted upon in certain ways.) Thanks to such linkages, anything in Smith's appearance, bearing, or behavior that could plausibly be attributed to his being upset or delighted may be traced farther to Dewey's having won.

No doubt it is useful to theorize in terms of counterfactuals that

---

1 Granted, one may speak of Smith as delighted about "the possibility that Dewey will be elected." But that can be paraphrased, "Smith is delighted (about the fact) that it is possible that Dewey will be elected." Note that such a paraphrase would not work for "Smith dreads the possibility that Dewey will be elected"; that is, "Smith dreads the fact that it is possible that Dewey will be elected."

so link a person's demeanor to the world, *when one can.* But often such connections are simply wanting. For one thing, emotions are often founded on mistake. Since Dewey was in fact *not* elected, one cannot link Smith's state to Dewey's having won. Even supposing that Dewey *had* been elected, Smith's belief, and hence his emotion and its behavioral train, may not have borne any causal or counterfactual connection to that event or state of affairs. Moreover, even where there is such a connection, it would seem a difficult feat of theorizing to establish its existence. Surely the safe and easy thing to do, and hence the more common thing to do, would be to attribute only belief, and to peg the anger or the delight onto that, leaving open the further questions whether Smith's belief is true and whether it constitutes knowledge. The question remains, then: Why is so strong an epistemic attribution, along with the strong causal or counterfactual implications it carries with it, *standardly* implicit in most attributions of emotion – and, indeed, in attributions of reasons as well? Why, in other words, is it the demotion to *mere belief* that requires a special circumlocution, rather than the promotion to knowledge? The problem is to explain *the normality of knowledge* in folk psychology.

In the remainder of this chapter, as a postscript to my discussion of the emotions, I sketch an account of folk psychology that would explain the normality of knowledge. I cannot claim that my account is adequately drawn, or that it would answer all other demands one might properly make, or that I have measured it against the salient alternatives (although no existing account of folk psychology even addresses the issue). I offer it as a stopgap.

KNOWLEDGE BY DEFAULT

One might have thought the attribution of knowledge to require a higher level of sophistication than the attribution of belief. For in attributing knowledge one attributes belief, *and then some*: justified undefeated belief, a reliable belief-producing mechanism, or the like. That *may* be true of attributions of knowledge in the "full-blooded" sense of the term 'knowledge'; or, alternatively, in the full-blooded sense of the term 'attribution.' But there are some attributions of knowledge (with whatever qualification, if any, needs to be made) that bespeak not sophistication but rather the *lack* of it – or, at least, failure to use the competence one has. The reason is that one may attribute knowledge to a person *by default*.

Suppose that in attempting to predict, explain, or understand O's behavior S fails to consider whether O might be ignorant of, or have differing beliefs about, some of the things S is certain of himself. The failure might be due to laziness, to thoughtless egocentrism, or to some other intellectual lapse. It might instead be due to lack of the relevant conceptual sophistication or competence: a lack of *the very concept of belief*. One may have failed to develop the capacity to *represent* differences in belief or the further capacity to *make allowances for* such differences in predicting or explaining behavior. Thus the possibility that another might, say, be ignorant of some of the things one is certain of, for example, that she might not be "in a position to know," could not enter one's calculations. I grant that a person who lacks the concept of belief lacks also the concept of *knowledge*. Thus I would not want to say that default attributions of knowledge are applications of the concept of knowledge. Nevertheless, given a certain methodology for predicting and explaining the behavior of others, to fail to make allowances for O's false or differing belief might be *methodologically equivalent* to attributing knowledge to O; that is, might have the same effect as a knowledge attribution in any attempt to explain or predict O's behavior. In that case, such failure may be said to constitute *an attribution, by default, of knowledge*.

This could not be so, of course, if in default of explicit attributions of belief there were nothing else to fill its methodological role: for then the absence of such attributions would leave one without any means for explanation and prediction. What is required is a methodology that, in default of explicit attributions of belief, fills "cognitive" slots in a way that is essentially *egocentric*. We typically explain *our own* present actions by direct appeal to "the facts," using forms of speech that imply knowledge: not "I am doing this because I believe that *p*" but, rather, "I am doing this because *p*," or "My reason for doing this is that *p*." Where factive emotions are concerned we typically specify what we ourselves are emoting about by citing the appropriate facts, again using forms of speech that imply knowledge: not "I am annoyed because I believe that *p*" but, rather, "I am annoyed about the fact that *p*," "I am annoyed that

131

p," "that p annoys me," or "I am annoyed because p."[2] Now, suppose that in default of explicit attributions of belief to others one simply reverted to this factive mode of explanation and prediction, filling cognitive slots by direct appeal to "the facts" (i.e., the facts as *we* take them to be). Then failing to attribute belief would indeed be methodologically equivalent to attributing knowledge. For such a methodology, knowledge, attributed by default, is the normal epistemic condition of others; mere belief is the noted exception.

There is some evidence that folk psychology is indeed *default-egocentric*, reverting to egocentric and thus factive forms of expression when no allowance is made for false or differing beliefs. Very young children give verbal expression to predictions and explanations of the behavior of others. Yet up to about the age of four they evidently lack the concept of belief, or at least the capacity to make allowances for false or differing beliefs. Instead they simply fill all "cognitive" slots with *the facts* – the "actual" facts, what *they* take to be the facts (as we, with our adult conceptual scheme, might put it). Evidence of this can be teased out by presenting children with stories and dramatizations that involve dramatic irony: where we the audience know something important that the protagonist doesn't know. (Such an experiment was carried out in Austria by Wimmer and Perner [1983]. They credit three philosophers – Bennett, Dennett, and Harman – with suggesting the experimental paradigm. The philosophers had suggested the paradigm, each independently, in response to Premack and Woodruff [1978] as a way of testing whether *chimpanzees* have a theory of mind.)

In one such story (illustrated with puppets) the puppet-child Maxi puts his chocolate in the box and goes out to play. While he is out, his mother transfers the chocolate to the cupboard. Where will Maxi look for the chocolate when he comes back? In the box, says the five-year-old, pointing to the miniature box on the puppet stage: a good prediction of a sort we ordinarily take for granted. (That is, after all, where the chocolate had been before it was, without Maxi's knowledge, transferred to the cupboard.) But the child of three to four years has a different response: Verbally or by pointing, the child indicates the cupboard. (That is, after all, where the choc-

2 The last of these may, of course, be read with or without the knowledge implication.

132

olate is to be found, isn't it?) Suppose Maxi wants to mislead his big brother to the *wrong* place. Where will he lead him? The five-year-old indicates the cupboard, where (unbeknownst to Maxi) the chocolate actually is; often accompanying the response with what is described as "an ironical smile." The *younger* child indicates, incorrectly, the box (Wimmer and Perner 1976).[3]

From this and other experiments it appears that in normal children between ages four and five there is a cognitive development that vastly enhances their capacity to predict the behavior of others. (Although retarded children with Down's syndrome undergo such development as well, autistic children even of fairly normal IQ clearly do not [Baron-Cohen, Leslie, and Frith 1985]. Their deficit is discussed later.) The child develops the ability to predict behavioral failures – such as failure to look in the right place, failure to mislead another to the wrong place – that result from *cognitive* failures, that is, false beliefs. At an earlier age children predict as if everything known to themselves were known to the other; which is to say, they *fail to make allowances* for what the other isn't in a position to know. One may say that young children attribute knowledge – by default – before they have learned to attribute belief.

The significance of this for the attribution of factive emotions is obvious. If knowledge may be attributed by default, even by one who lacks the concept of belief, then factive emotions may also be attributed by one who lacks the concept of belief. Young children who lack the capacity to represent and make allowances for differences in the way the world may be "seen" *might*, nonetheless, be able to attribute regret or delight, indeed, to attribute regret or delight with a specific content, for example, that the chocolate is in the box. (The same might also be true of autistic children and, indeed, may have been true of early *Homo sapiens* and their hominid precursors.) Their capacity to predict and explain behavior would, of course, be narrowly constrained, for they would be unable to recognize or even to conceptualize emotions founded on false beliefs. And they would be highly prone to error in the attributions they do make, since they assume by default that others will know what they know. (The error rate, relatively low when attributions

3 My account simplifies the experiment and the results; but not, I think, unconscionably.

133

are made within a close-knit, like-thinking family or community, would shoot up drastically when aliens enter the scene.) I am not saying that children do in fact make such attributions before they have acquired the concept of belief: I do not know. What I am saying is that there appears to be no conceptual barrier to such precociousness. It would be interesting to see if they – very young children and autistic children – do make such restricted, error-prone attributions. It would also be interesting to see if the *epistemic* emotions must not, by contrast, await the acquisition of the concept of belief.[4]

If a knowledge attribution is implicit also in rational explanation, then a child or a precursor of *Homo sapiens* who lacked the competence to attribute beliefs might nonetheless be capable of explaining another's behavior in terms of the agent's reason(s) for acting. As in the case of emotion attributions, such explanations would often fall wide of the mark, particularly when aliens enter the scene. It would begin to appear that the concept of belief is merely an adjunct to folk psychology – albeit one that vastly increases its predictive power.

If *infantile* folk psychology is universally egocentric and factive, as the Wimmer and Perner experiments suggest, by what means are its limitations overcome? By what methodology does a *mature* folk psychology explain and predict behavior? In particular, how does one move from explanations and predictions in terms of "the facts" to explanations and predictions in terms of false or differing beliefs – "the facts" from another's "perspective"? Does the four-year-old's great cognitive leap forward consist (as many philosophers would seem committed to saying) in the acquisition of a set of laws that putatively govern the inner workings of the human mind?

These are the questions I shall *begin* to address in the remainder of this final chapter.

PREDICTING ONE'S OWN BEHAVIOR

Discussions of the nature of folk psychology and of its adequacy, particularly as a basis for predictions of overt human behavior,

---

4 I am speaking of attributions of fearing that *p*, not attributions of "the state of fear." See Chapter 4 for the distinction.

ought to begin by dividing the question: *one's own* behavior or *another's?* behavior in the *immediate* or in the *distant* future? behavior under *existing* conditions or under specified *hypothetical* conditions? For such a division uncovers a little-known and unappreciated success story: our prodigious ability to foretell what we ourselves are "about to do" in the (actual) immediate future. We have in this department a success rate that surely would be the envy of any behavioral or neurobehavioral science.

The trick, of course, is not to predict until one has "made up one's mind" what to do: then one simply declares what one "intends" to do. We display our confidence in the *predictive relia-bility* of these declarations by the way we formulate them: One typically says, not "I intend now to _____" but simply "I shall now _____" or "I will now _____." Somehow, in learning to "express our (immediate) intention" we learn to utter sentences that, construed as statements about our own future behavior, prove to be extremely reliable.[5] For example:

> I shall now pour some coffee.
> I shall now pick up the cup.
> I shall now drink the coffee.

Such predictions, if not quite as reliable as 'Night will follow day' or 'This chair will hold my weight,' are at least among the most reliable one is likely to make. Of course, one would have to allow for unforeseen interventions by "nature" (sudden paralysis, a coffee cup glued to the table) and for ignorance (the stuff you pour and drink isn't coffee). But that seems a realistic limitation on any *psychological* basis for prediction.

Normally, apart from these conditions, the only errors occur when something "makes us change our mind": The phone rings before we have poured the coffee, we see that the stuff isn't coffee,

---

5 The qualifying phrase is added because I am concerned with assertive reliability, not commissive reliability: that of predictions, rather than that of promises, vows, and expressions of intention. Construing "I shall now *X*" as a mere expression of intention, if the speaker does not *X* he will have "failed to carry out" his intention: His action would in a (nonmoral) sense be "at fault." Construing it as a mere prediction, on the other hand, it would be the prediction that is "at fault," not the action. To use Searle's distinction (derived from Anscombe), declarations of intention have a world-to-word "direction of fit," whereas predictions and other "assertive" speech acts have a word-to-world direction of fit (Searle 1983). This distinction does not affect the essential point being made here.

and so on.) A plausible explanation of this reliability is that our declarations of immediate intention are causally tied to some actual precursor of behavior: perhaps tapping into the brain's updated behavioral "plans" or into "executive commands" that are about to guide the relevant motor sequences.[6] In any case, these everyday predictions of behavior seem to have an anchor in psychological reality.

One might have thought all predictions of human behavior to be inferences from theoretical premises about beliefs, desires, and emotions, together with laws connecting these with behavior: laws of the form 'if A is in states S_1, S_2, S_3, and so on, and conditions C_1, C_2, C_3 obtain, then A will (or will probably) do X.' Thus one would have a *deductive-nomological* or *inductive-nomological* basis for prediction. This is plainly not so: Declarations of immediate intention – "I shall now X" – are not products of inference from such premises.

Moreover, if they were, one could not account for either their predictive reliability or our *confidence* in their predictive reliability. We are not self-omniscient: We do not keep tabs on all of the relevant beliefs and attitudes, and *a fortiori* we do not keep a *reliable* inventory of these. But even if we knew all the relevant beliefs and attitudes, our predictions would at best be qualified and chancy. Folk psychology, on most accounts, doesn't specify a deterministic system; it specifies only the probable or "typical" effects of mental states. Using it as my basis, I should have to qualify my predictions by saying, for example, "*Typically*, I would now pick up the cup." And actions that are *atypical, exceptional*, or *out of character* – my wearing a tie to class, or my heckling the commencement speaker – would defy prediction altogether, even seconds before I take action. Whereas in fact I feel confident that I can predict what I am about to do now, whether the act is typical or not; and my confidence seems well-founded: I predict imminent atypical actions about as reliably as any others.

Although they are not based on nomological reasoning, declarations of immediate intention – these ultrareliable predictors of behavior – are often products of *practical* reasoning: reasoning that

6 A further possibility is that a degree of normative commitment is added by the *declaration* of an intention, even if it is announced only to oneself: One is then motivated to *mold* one's behavior to the declared intention. This was suggested to me by Brian McLaughlin.

provides the basis for a decision *to do* something.[7] "I shall now write a letter" may express a decision based on certain salient facts (a student asked me to write a letter of recommendation), salient norms and values (I have a duty to write letters for good students who request letters, and she's a good student), and a background of other facts, norms, and values that I am unable to list exhaustively. The important point is that declarations of the form 'I shall now do *x*' offer a bridge between such practical reasoning and prediction.

This bridge introduces a very interesting possibility: that of using *simulated* practical reasoning as a *predictive* device. First of all, it is easy to see how, by simulating the appropriate practical reasoning, we can extend our capacity for self-prediction in a way that would enable us to predict *our own behavior in hypothetical situations*. Thus I might predict, for example, what I would do if, right now, the screen of the word processor I am working on were to go blank; or what I would do if I were now to hear footsteps coming from the basement.

To simulate the appropriate practical reasoning I can engage in a kind of *pretend play*: pretend that the indicated conditions *actually obtain*, with all other conditions remaining (so far as is logically possible and physically probable) as they presently stand; then – continuing the make-believe – try to "make up my mind" what to do given these (modified) conditions. I imagine, for instance, a lone modification of the actual world: the sound of footsteps from the basement.[8] Then I ask, in effect, "What shall I do now?" And I answer with a declaration of immediate intention, "I shall now _____." This, too, is only feigned. But it is not feigned on a tabula rasa, as if at random: Rather, the declaration of immediate intention appears to be formed in the way a *decision* is formed, *constrained* by the (pretended) "fact" that there is the sound of footsteps from the basement, the (*un*pretended) fact that such a sound would now be unlikely if there weren't an intruder in the basement, the (*un*pretended) awfulness of there being an intruder in the basement, and so forth.

---

7 More precisely, *what is expressed by* these declarations is often a product of practical reasoning.
8 Imagery is not always needed in such simulations. For example, I need no imagery to simulate having a million dollars in the bank. Mere supposition would be enough.

What I have performed is a kind of *practical simulation*, a simulated deciding *what to do*. Some simulated decisions in hypothetical situations include acting out, for instance, rehearsals and drills. The kind I am interested in, however, suppress the behavioral output. One reports the simulated decision as a *hypothetical prediction*: a prediction of what I would do in the specified hypothetical circumstances, other things being as they are. For example: "If I were now to hear footsteps from the basement, (probably) I would reach for the telephone and call 911."[9]

I noted earlier that one could not account for either the *confidence* or the *reliability* with which I predict what I am about to do now, if such predictions were based on attributions of beliefs, desires, and the like, together with laws. The same holds for *hypothetical* self-predictions. Once again I don't know enough about my beliefs and desires; and the laws would at best yield only the *typical* effects of those states, anyway.[10] In real life we sometimes surprise ourselves with *atypical* responses: "I certainly wouldn't have thought I'd react that way!" Practical simulation imitates real life in this respect, giving us the capacity to surprise ourselves *before* we confront the actual situation. If I pretend *realistically* that there is an intruder in the house, I *might* find myself surprisingly brave – or cowardly.[11]

PREDICTING THE BEHAVIOR OF OTHERS

In one type of hypothetical *self*-prediction the hypothetical situation is one that some *other* person has actually been in, or at least is described as having been in. The task is to answer the question 'What would *I* do in *that* person's situation?' For example, chess players report that when playing against a human opponent or even against a computer, they visualize the board from the other side,

---

9 Contrast "I would (if such a situation were now to arise) reach for the telephone and dial 911," uttered as a declaration of conditional intention. The difference can be partially explicated in terms of "direction of fit."

10 Granted, if one were to do some of the pretending out loud, one might say, for example, "I believe someone has broken into the house." But such a verbalization has a role in practical, not nomological, reasoning: One is articulating a possible basis for action, not giving a state description that is to be plugged into laws that bridge between internal states and behavior.

11 Needless to say, like any attempt to explain or predict one's own behavior, this may be corrupted by prejudice or self-deception.

taking the opposing pieces for their own and vice versa. Further, they pretend that their *reasons for action* have shifted accordingly: Whereas previously the fact that a move would make White's queen vulnerable would constitute a reason *for* making the move, it now becomes a reason *against*; and so on. Thus transported in imagination, they "make up their mind what to do." *That*, they conclude, is what *I* would do (have done). They are "putting themselves in the other's shoes," in one sense of that expression; that is, they project themselves into the other's *situation*, but without any attempt to project themselves into, as we say, the other's "mind."

A prediction of how I would act in the other's situation is not, of course, a prediction of how the other will act – unless the other should happen to be, in causally relevant respects, a *replica* of me. But people claim also that by "putting themselves in the other's shoes," in a somewhat different sense of that expression, they can predict the *other's* behavior. As in the case of hypothetical self-prediction, the methodology essentially involves *deciding what to do*; but, extended to people of "minds" different from one's own, this is not the same as deciding *what I myself would do*. One tries to make *adjustments for relevant differences*. In chess, for example, a player would make not only the imaginative shifts required for predicting "what *I* would do in his shoes" but the further shifts required for predicting what *he* will do in his shoes. To this purpose the player might, for instance, simulate a lower level of play, trade one set of idiosyncrasies for another, and above all pretend ignorance of *his own* (actual) intentions. Army generals, salespeople, and detectives claim to do this sort of thing. Sherlock Holmes expresses the point with characteristic modesty:

You know my methods in such cases, Watson. I put myself in the man's place, and, having first gauged his intelligence, I try to imagine how I should myself have proceeded under the same circumstances. In this case the matter was simplified by Brunton's intelligence being quite first-rate, so that it was unnecessary to make any allowance for the personal equation, as the astronomers have dubbed it. (Doyle 1894)

The procedure serves cooperative as well as competitive ends: Not to go far afield, bridge players claim they can project themselves into their *partner's* shoes.

The general idea of putting oneself in the other's shoes is supported by the hermeneutic tradition, particularly by Collingwood (1946) in his notion of historical reenactment and Continental ex-

139

ponents of *Verstehen*, roughly defined as "empathetic understanding" (see Schutz 1962, 1967; von Wright 1971:chap. 1).[12] But little attention has been given to prediction. Nor have these authors appreciated the methodological importance of hypothesis testing and experimentation in practical simulation: the fact that at its heart is a type of reasoning I characterize as *hypotheticopractical*. Finally, they have not tried to explain the very concept of belief in terms of practical simulation, as I shall.

AN EXAMPLE OF HYPOTHETICODEDUCTIVE REASONING

I shall illustrate with an extended example of hypotheticopractical reasoning. You and a friend sit down at a table in a fashionable international restaurant in New York. The waiter approaches. He greets you effusively in what strikes you as a Slavic language. He says nothing to your friend. You do not speak any Slavic language.

You wish to understand the waiter's behavior. You wish also to predict his future behavior, given various responses you might make to his greeting. As a first step, you shift spatiotemporal perspectives – you are standing over there now, where the waiter is, not sitting here.

In some cases, shifting spatiotemporal perspectives might be enough: for example, for predicting, or explaining, the behavior of a person you see in the path of an oncoming car. This would be woefully inadequate for the restaurant example, of course. As a further experiment, you might switch institutional roles. You suppose (and perhaps imagine) yourself to be a waiter, waiting on a customer sitting here in this restaurant. Such counterfactual suppositions raise difficult questions. For example, shall you suppose yourself to be a waiter who has, say, read Quine (as in fact you have)? Shall you suppose the *customer* to have read Quine?[13] Fortunately, one does not ordinarily have to ask these questions, since they would make no difference in one's behavior in this situation; and when they do make a difference, the situation is likely to alert one to their relevance.

Donning your waiter's uniform is clearly not enough: To have

12 Closer to my own view is Morton (1980:chap. 3) on the uses of imagination in understanding another's behavior.
13 As Quine has noted, "Casting our real selves thus in unreal roles, we do not generally know how much reality to hold constant" (1960:92).

what you see as a basis for greeting the customer in a Slavic language, supposing you could, you should have to alter other facts. As a first stab, you might see yourself as an émigré from a Slavic country, working as a waiter. You seem to recognize the customer: He is a countryman of yours who used to eat at the restaurant many years ago. It pleases him, as you recall, to be greeted in the native tongue. That would be a reason for doing so. There being no reasons not to, that is what you do – in make-believe.

Other modifications of the world would lead to the same decision. Suppose that, before the restaurant episode, you had read a cheap spy thriller. Under its corrosive influence you hypothesize as follows: You are a counterintelligence agent posing as a waiter. The customer you are waiting on is a known spy from a Slavic country, and there is good reason to get him to reveal that he knows the language of this country. One way to do this is to watch his reaction when you address him in the language of his country. Given this background, you might indeed address him in that language, if you could.

To choose between the two hypotheses would require further tests. Suppose that in your real role of customer, you look puzzled and respond, "I don't understand that language. You must be making a mistake." On the countryman hypothesis, the waiter will probably apologize – in English – and explain that he had mistaken you for someone else. On the counterspy hypothesis, he may either persist in speaking in the foreign tongue or turn to more subtle devices for getting the customer to reveal his knowledge of the language. If, in fact, the waiter apologizes, the counterspy hypothesis will have suffered one perhaps small defeat.

Ideally, the hypothesis testing would continue until the subject appeared to be, as it were, *the puppet of one's (simulated) intentions.* In actuality, when I persist in my effort to find a pretend world in which the other's behavior would accord with my intentions, I usually find myself, after a number of errors, "tracking" the other person fairly well, forming a fairly stable pretend world for that person. Of course, I cannot predict or anticipate exactly what he will do, to any fine-grained description. But, by and large, I shall not be very much surprised very often, at least in matters important to interpersonal coordination.

No matter how long we go on testing hypotheses, we shall not have tried out *all* candidate explanations of the waiter's behavior.

Perhaps some of the unexamined candidates would have done at least as well as the one we settle for, if we settle: perhaps indefinitely many of them would have. But these would be "farfetched," we say intuitively. Therein we exhibit our inertial bias: The less "fetching" (or "stretching," as actors say) we have to do to track the other's behavior, the better. We tend to *feign* only when necessary, only when something in the other's behavior doesn't fit. This inertial bias may be thought of as a "least effort" principle: the "principle of least pretending." It explains why, other things being equal, we shall prefer the less radical departure from the "real" world – that is, from what we ourselves take to be the world.

Within a close-knit community, where people have a vast common fund of "facts," as well as shared norms and values, only a minimum of pretending would be called for. (In the limit case – a replica – the distinction noted earlier between 'what *I would* do in the other's situation' and 'what *the other will* do in his situation' would indeed vanish, except as a formal or conceptual distinction: What I would do and what the other will do would invariably coincide.) A person transplanted into an alien culture might have to do a great deal of pretending to explain and predict the behavior of those around him. Indeed, one might eventually learn to *begin* all attempts at explanation and prediction with a stereotypic set of adjustments: pretending that dancing causes rain, that grasshoppers taste better than beefsteak, that blue-eyed should never marry brown-eyed, and so on. This "default" set of world modifications might be said to constitute one's "generalizations" about the alien culture.

Whether or not practical simulation begins with such stereotypes, it does not essentially involve (as one might think) an implicit *comparison to oneself*. Although it does essentially involve *deciding what to do*, that, as I have noted, is not the same as deciding *what I myself would do*. To predict another's behavior I may have to pretend that there is an Aryan race, that it is metaphysically the master race, and that I belong to it; finally, that I was born in Germany of German stock between 1900 and 1920. To make decisions within such a pretend world is not to decide what *I myself* would do, much less to know reliably what *I myself* would do, "in that situation." First, it is not possible for *me* to be in that situation, if indeed it is a possible *situation* (for anyone); second, it is not possible for me even to *believe* myself to be in that situation – not,

142

at least, without such vast changes in my beliefs and attitudes as to make all prediction unreliable. Hence I cannot be making an implicit *comparison to myself*.[14]

I do not deny that explanations are often couched in terms of *beliefs, desires*, and the like. Or that predictions are often made on the basis of attributions of such states. This is particularly so in discourse about *other* people or about oneself at times other than the present. Moreover, as functionalist accounts of folk psychology have emphasized, common discourse about beliefs and other mental states presupposes that they enter into a multitude of causal and nomological relations. I don't want to deny this either. A particular instance or "token" of belief, such as Smith's belief that Dewey won the election, may be (given a background of other beliefs, desires, etc.) *a cause of* Smith's doing something (joining the Republican Party) or undergoing something (being glad, being upset); it may have been *caused by* his reading in the newspapers that Dewey won and his believing that newspapers are reliable in such matters, or by his having taken a hallucinogenic drug.

There are, in addition, certain formally describable regularities that might be formulated as laws of typical causation: for instance, a belief that p and a belief that (if p then q) will typically cause a belief that q; a desire that p and a belief that (p if and only if I bring it about that q) will typically cause a desire to bring it about that q. And there are more specific regularities that obtain for particular individuals, classes, communities, or cultures: When some tennis players believe their opponents aren't playing their best they typically get angry; when members of a certain tribe see a cloud they think inhabited by an animal spirit they typically prepare for the hunt. And sometimes it helps to remember such regularities when predicting or explaining behavior – even one's own.

One mustn't apply such generalizations too mechanically, how-

14 Nozick (1981) seems to miss this point in his account of *Verstehen* as "a special form of inference by analogy, in that I am the thing to which he is analogous." He argues that the inference depends on two empirical correlations: "that he acts as I would, and that I would as I (on the basis of imaginative projection) think I would" (1981:636). Nozick's mistake is to think it relevant to ask, and, indeed, essential as the inferential link, how I would in fact behave in the other's shoes.

ever. For there are indefinitely many circumstances, not exhaustively specifiable in advance, in which these general or specific regularities fail to hold. Generalizations that do not explicitly concern only "typical" instances should be understood to contain implicit *ceteris paribus* clauses. (This point is developed, along with much else that is congenial, in Putnam 1978:Lecture VI.) How does one know how to recognize atypical situations or to expand the *ceteris paribus* clause? An answer is ready at hand. As long as one applies these generalizations *in the context of practical simulation*, the unspecifiable constraints on *one's own* practical reasoning would enable one to delimit the application of these rules. This gives one something to start with: As one learns more about others, of course, one learns how to modify these constraints in applying generalizations to them.

Moreover, the *interpretation* of such generalizations, as indeed of all common discourse about beliefs and other mental states, remains open to question. In the remainder of this chapter I sketch and at least begin to defend a way of interpreting ordinary discourse about *beliefs* in terms of pretend play and practical simulation. The idea isn't wholly new. In *Word and Object*, Quine explained indirect quotation and the ascription of propositional attitudes in terms of what he called "an essentially dramatic act":

We project ourselves into what, from his remarks and other indications, we imagine the speaker's state of mind to have been, and then we say what, in our language, is natural and relevant for us in the state thus feigned. (1960:92)

That is, we first try to simulate, by a sort of pretending, another's state of mind; then we just "speak our mind." In Quine's view, this is essentially an exercise in translation and heir to all its problems. Stephen Stich develops the idea further, using a device introduced by Davidson: In saying, for example, "Smith believes that Dewey won," one utters the content sentence 'Dewey won,' pretending to be asserting it oneself, as if performing a little skit (1983). To ascribe such a belief to Smith is to say that he is in a state *similar* to the one that might typically be expected to underlie that utterance – had it not been produced by way of playacting.

As Stich portrays the playacting device, it is merely a device for producing a specimen utterance that, in turn, is used to specify a particular theoretical state. The attribution of such a state is sup-

144

posed to play a role in nomological reasoning roughly analogous to that of attributions of theoretical states in the physical sciences, and in that role to serve in the tasks of explaining and predicting the object's behavior.[15] Rather than treating the observer as an *agent* in his own right, as one who might form intentions to *act* on the basis of pretend inputs, it calls upon him merely to *speak* as he would given those inputs.

Stich's assumption that the methodological context for such attributions is nomological reasoning leads him, I believe, to misrepresent the role of pretending in folk psychology. I shall sketch very briefly a different role for pretending in belief attribution. On this account, the methodological context for such attributions is not nomological reasoning but practical simulation.

A chess player who visualizes the board from his opponent's point of view might find it helpful to *verbalize* from that point of view – to assert, for example, "My queen is in danger." Stepping into Smith's shoes, I might say, "Dewey won the election." Such assertions may then be used as premises of simulated practical inference. But wouldn't it be a great advantage to us practical simulators if we could *pool our resources*? We'll simulate Smith *together*, cooperatively, advising one another as to what premises or inputs to practical reasoning would work best for a simulation of Smith – that is, give the best predictions and the most stable explanations, explanations that won't have to be revised in the light of new evidence. Of course, I couldn't come *straight out* with the utterance "Dewey won." I need to flag the utterance as one being uttered *from within a Smith-simulation mode*, and addressed to *your* Smith-simulation mode. I might do this by saying something like the following:

1. Let's do a Smith simulation. Ready? *Dewey won the election.*

The same task might be accomplished by saying:

2. *Smith believes that* Dewey won the election.

My suggestion is that (2) be read as saying the same thing as (1), though less explicitly.

15 To do this job properly, it would have to meet certain standards of objectivity. And Stich argues with considerable force that it cannot. For it never frees itself fully from the subjectivity it necessarily begins with, the speaker relativity that is built into the ascription of content.

It is worth noting that, unlike Stich, I am not characterizing belief as a relation to any linguistic entity or speech act, such as a sentence or an assertion. Nor, as far as I can see, does my suggestion involve explicating the contents of beliefs in terms of possible worlds. Rather than specifying, *in a standard nonpretending mode of speech*, a set of possible worlds, one says something about the *actual* world – albeit *in a nonstandard, pretending mode of speech*. Needless to say, the exposition and defense of this account of belief are much in need of further development. But one can see that, given the principle of least pretending mentioned earlier, our belief attributions would be in accord with something like the principle of charity put forward by Quine and Davidson: roughly, that one should prefer a translation that maximizes truth and rationality. More precisely, our attributions would conform to an improved version of this principle: Grandy's more general "principle of humanity," according to which one should prefer a translation on which "the imputed pattern of relations among beliefs, desires, and the world be as similar to our own as possible" (1973:443).

If I am right, to attribute a belief to another person is to make an assertion, to state something as a fact, *within the context of practical simulation*. Mastery of the concept of belief would not be a matter of learning laws or generalizations. It would be simply the ability to *take something as a fact* – and, typically, also to *state* something as a fact, to make an assertion – *within the context of practical simulation*. This would account for the results of the Wimmer–Perner experiment described earlier in this chapter. Suppose that at age four the child normally learns to harness her capacity for pretend play for the purpose of practical simulation, and thus acquires the ability to take (and to state) something as a fact within the context of practical simulation. That would give her the capacity to overcome an initial egocentric limitation to the *actual facts* (i.e., the facts as *she* sees them) in her explanations and predictions of the behavior of others. One would expect a change of just the sort exhibited by the children studied in the Wimmer–Perner experiment.

It is the position of many philosophers, however, that commonsense terms such as 'believes' are *theoretical* terms, the meanings of which are fixed in the same way as theoretical terms in general: by the set of laws and generalizations in which they figure. This view is widely (but not universally) assumed in functionalist accounts of folk psychology. (It is the offspring of the dispositional theories that were popular in the days of philosophical behaviorism.) Presumably, mastery of the concept of belief would then be a matter of internalizing a sufficiently large number of laws or generalizations in which the term 'belief' (and related verb forms) occurs. The term 'belief' would be used in something like the way biologists used the term 'gene' before the discovery of DNA.[16]

But suppose that mastery of the concept of belief did consist in learning or in some manner internalizing a system of laws and generalizations concerning belief. One would in that case expect that *before* internalizing this system, the child would simply be unable to predict or explain human action. And *after* internalizing the system the child could deal indifferently with actions caused by *true* beliefs and actions caused by *false* beliefs. It is hard to see how the semantical question could be relevant: how children might come to grasp and use the notion of true belief more precociously than that of false belief. The distinct developmental stages revealed in the Wimmer–Perner experiment would be quite unexpected and difficult to explain.

There is further evidence to support my account of belief attribution. Practical simulation involves the capacity for a certain kind of systematic pretending. It is well known that *autistic* children suffer a striking deficit in the capacity for pretend play. In addition, they are often said to "treat people and objects alike": They fail to treat others as subjects, as having "points of view" distinct from their own. This failure is confirmed by their performance in prediction tests like the one I have just described. A version of the Wimmer–Perner test was administered to autistic children of ages *six to sixteen* by a team of psychologists (Baron-Cohen, Leslie, and Frith 1985). *Almost all* these children gave the wrong answer – the three-year-old's answer. This indicates a highly specific deficit, not one in general intelligence. Although many autistic children are also mentally retarded, those tested were mostly in the average or borderline IQ range. Yet children with Down's syndrome, with IQ levels

16 But a functionalist might wish to say that whereas the correct explication of the concept requires that one cite such laws, mastery of the concept, that is, the ability to use it, does not require that one have internalized such laws. Thus, some functionalists might even be prepared to embrace something like my account of belief attributions. This possibility (or something close to it) was pointed out to me independently by Larry Davis and Sydney Shoemaker. I am inclined to think that this would be an uneasy alliance, but I confess I don't (as yet) have the arguments to persuade anybody who might think otherwise.

substantially below that range, suffered no deficit: Almost all gave the right answer. My account of belief would predict that only those children who can engage in pretend play can master the concept of belief.[17] Autistic children do at least as well as normal children in their comprehension of *mechanical* operations – a distinct blow to any functionalists who might think mastery of the concept of belief to consist in the acquisition of a theory of the functional organization of a mechanism.

I suspect that, once acquired, the capacity for practical simulation operates primarily at a subverbal level, enabling us to *anticipate* in our own actions the behavior of others, although we are unable to say *what* it is that we anticipate or *why*. The *self-reported* pretending I have described would then be only the tip of the iceberg. Something like it may happen quite regularly and without our knowledge: Our decision-making or practical-reasoning system gets partially disengaged from its "natural" inputs and fed instead with suppositions and images (or their "subpersonal" or "subdoxastic" counterparts). Given these artificial pretend inputs, the system then "makes up its mind" what to do. Because the system is being run off-line, as it were, disengaged also from its natural output systems, its "decision" isn't actually executed but, rather, ends up as an anticipation, perhaps just an unconscious *motor* anticipation, of the other's behavior.

One possibility is that the readiness for practical simulation is a prepackaged "module" called upon automatically in the perception of other human beings. One might even speculate that such a module makes its first appearance in the useful tendency many mammals have of turning their eyes toward the target of another's gaze. Thus the very sight of human eyes might *require* us to simulate at least their spatial perspective – and to this extent, at least, to put ourselves in the other's shoes. This would give substance to the notion that we perceive one another primarily as *subjects*: as world centers rather

17 My account is close in many respects to the theory the investigators were themselves testing in the autism experiment. This is presented in A. M. Leslie, "Pretense and Representation in Infancy: The Origins of 'Theory of Mind.' " (I thank Dr. Leslie for making available a copy of his paper.) Leslie's thesis is that the capacity for pretend play and the ability to attribute mental states involve a common cognitive mechanism (namely, a decoupling from primary representations). My thesis is that a form of pretend play is actually required for the attribution of mental states; from which it follows that whatever mechanism underlies pretend play is also implicated in mental attribution.

than as objects in the world. It is pleasant to speculate that the phenomenology of *the Other* – particularly the Sartrean idea that consciousness of the Other robs us of our own perspective – might have such humble beginnings.

PRACTICAL SIMULATION AND EMOTIONS

In the remaining pages I discuss some ways in which a simulational account of folk psychology might bear specifically on the recognition and attribution of emotions. A full simulational account of these matters would require that I first give a simulational account of attributions of wishes and desires. I shall not attempt this here. Following standard practice in recent treatments of folk psychology, I have focused on belief attribution. Some readers might surmise, particularly from some of my asides in Chapter 6, that I equate desiring with *believing desirable* – and thus that I might deem it unnecessary to give a separate account of desire attribution. This would be far from the truth: It is because of the special complexities of desire attribution that I venture no brief simulational account. (Some of these complexities are stated and discussed in Gordon 1986a and 1986b).

Pending an account of wish and desire attribution, we can spell out at least some of the ways in which a simulational conception of folk psychology bears on the emotions. There is, indeed, some fairly direct fallout from a simulational account of belief attribution. In Chapter 2, I considered how one might attribute a factive emotion when there is (from one's own point of view) no "fact" for the emotion to be about. One could not say straightforwardly, for example, "Smith is upset (about the fact) that there are Martian spaceships circling the Earth," without risk of sounding crazy oneself. The usual maneuver, I suggested, would be to explain the emotion in terms of the subject's cognitive state, as in "Smith is upset because he believes that there are Martian spaceships circling the Earth." But in certain contexts, including fictional and clinical reports, it is convenient to adopt a convention of extreme charity, whereby one attributes mental states as if whatever the subject *believed* to be so he *knew* to be so. This pretense permits one to preserve factivity without endorsement: One may then say, for instance, "Smith is upset (about the fact) that there are Martian spaceships circling the Earth," without risk of sounding crazy oneself.

These two maneuvers now appear essentially the same. In either case, one asserts in a simulational mode of speech that there are Martian spaceships circling the Earth. The chief difference between the two maneuvers is that adopting the convention of extreme charity makes it unnecessary to signal each use of a simulational mode of speech by prefacing it with 'Smith believes that . . . '

To accommodate emotions, however, we must expand the notion of practical simulation. For in practical simulation, as described earlier in this chapter, the facts (actual or pretended) are used as premises in simulated practical reasoning. But the causal structures of emotions, as I endeavored to show in Chapter 6, are quite distinct from those exemplified in practical reasoning. In practical reasoning the "facts" that (given one's desires) form the basis for one's action speak in favor of so acting, for example, by showing the action to be instrumental to the end desired. But the "facts" that form the basis for one's emotion – such as wish-satisfying or wish-frustrating facts – do not correspondingly favor so emoting. Although one may be able to talk someone into, for example, being proud of his home by saying something positive about his being proud of his home, the standard form of argument (which reflects the causal structure of pride) is to say something positive about his home.

It seems quite natural to expand the notion of practical simulation to include simulation of the causal structures of the various emotions. By pretending (in supposition or imagination) to be in some hypothetical (contrary to fact) situation, we can predict not only our action in such a situation but also our emotional reaction to the situation. Moreover, we could hardly be reliable in predicting actions if we could not also predict emotional reactions. In explaining and predicting behavior one leaves lacunae, I argued in Chapter 1, if one neglects the emotions. Consider again the book-burning example: Smith's wife burned the book manuscript of Jones, the chairperson, who had been having an affair with Smith's husband. The fact that they were having an affair made her *want* to burn Jones's manuscript, but not by way of practical reasoning alone, not, for instance, because doing so would serve some further end (e.g., deter them from continuing the affair) or satisfy some principle (e.g., restore her honor, right a wrong). Pretending our situation to be in certain respects like hers we could easily hypothesize a quite different pathway between the fact and the action. For her situation was (among other things) one of wish-frustration: As we might express it, "Would that this affair *had not happened!*" This introduces a new range of possible connections with behavior. For example, we might do something injurious to one or both of the lovers (out of anger). But we might instead (or in addition) do something injurious to ourselves (out of shame); or we might hide the fact of the affair, or even hide ourselves, from others' eyes (out of embarrassment, perhaps compounded with shame). Further elaboration of the wish-frustration hypothesis would be required to complete the explanation: Was it wish-frustration of the sort required for anger? for shame? for embarrassment? Or we might do the elaboration in reverse: Was the behavior of the sort that might have been produced by anger? by shame? by embarrassment? Then, tentatively, we might hypothesize that the corresponding type of wish-frustration had caused the emotion.

The testing of hypotheses about another's emotion might involve more than *thought* experiments: Just as one devised ways to test the waiter's intentions, one can devise ways of testing the emotions of others. Often this takes the form of a test of the genuineness of another's apparent emotion. For example, a woman explains various aspects of her suitor's behavior by the hypothesis that she has (in his eyes) personal qualities he delights in; and she has never noticed any behavior that she regards as disconfirming this hypothesis. She wonders, however, if his delight is genuine, or at least genuinely about her personal qualities. The hackneyed story continues: She gives him to believe that she is not as wealthy as he had thought, then waits to see if his delight becomes less evident. Should he fail the test, she could not retain the hypothesis that his delight had been genuine, and genuinely about her personal qualities, without adding heroic and farfetched projective hypotheses.

EMPATHY AND THEORY

Simulation of the causal structures of emotions inevitably invites comparison to empathy. Psychologists have made some useful refinements of the initially vague notion of empathy that help us to refine such a comparison.[18] Some would identify empathy with vicarious affective response, wherein observation of another's emotion-arousing situation and emotion-manifesting behavior causes the same emotion (and, according to most accounts of empathy, the same emotional feeling) to be aroused in the observer. "The same emotion" is, of course, a problematic notion. Sharing the young wrestler's contagious joy over (his) having won the match, I do not become joyous over (my) having won the match. He is also proud of having won; but even though I might be said to feel his ("palpable") pride, it is, in a sense, his pride I feel: Because I bear no special relationship to him, I myself do not become proud of his victory. Although there is, apparently, such a thing as vicarious conditioning, in which observation of another's reaction to a stimulus actually conditions one to respond more or less similarly to similar stimuli, the vicarious affective responses more commonly identified with empathy are often characterized as "as if" responses, rather like the "as if" decisions described in my discussion of simulated practical reasoning earlier in this chapter. Thus, in my vicarious affective response to the wrestler's triumph I do not myself become proud but only "as if proud," or – in now familiar terms – proud in a simulational context. And although I may happen to be glad that he won and even joyous over his victory, my *vicarious* affective response is not one of actual gladness or joy but one of disengaged or "as if" gladness and joy – indeed, "as if" gladness and joy over something I myself accomplished, namely, (my) having won. For here I picture the wrestler's situation from his point of view, as one in which I am a young wrestler who has just won a match, and so on.

The notion of an "as if" emotion becomes more comprehensible if we suppose that, just as already envisaged in the case of our decision-making or practical-reasoning system, our emotion-producing system may be run off-line, disengaged from its natural input and output systems. Hypothesis testing would again be central to the methodology, whether such testing is carried out consciously or not. One would "try on" various emotions, seeking

18 I owe most of my acquaintance with recent psychological work on empathy to an unpublished doctoral dissertation by Maureen Osborne, presented in 1984 to the University of Missouri–St. Louis. The account that follows is highly selective and biased to present purposes; and I have omitted the many citations that even this sampling would require.

the best fit to the observed situation (with the appropriate spatiotemporal shifts, along with other "indexical" shifts) and the observed behavior, engaging in further pretending where necessary. But in such hypotheticoemotional reasoning one would not be concerned exclusively with matching the other's intentional behavior, for there are also nonintentional manifestations of various emotions, which are more or less standard, at least within a given culture. In seeking to match these nonintentional manifestations one may be aided by automatic mechanisms of various sorts. There is solid experimental evidence, for example, that in observing others we engage in subliminal muscular activity (measurable by electromyography) that mimics their facial expressions and overt bodily motions. Feedback from such motor mimicry is thought by some psychologists to be an important factor in the recognition of emotions in others. Such a mechanism could, indeed, preempt much of the hypothesis testing, often leaving only the specific content of the emotion to be determined by testing.

Allowance would have to be made, once again, for individual differences: for "the personal equation," as Sherlock Holmes called it. This would encompass differences in temperament, mood, and expressiveness, among others. It is notorious that some people are quicker to anger than others and that some have a lower threshold for positive emotions than others. The same person may have a threshold for a given emotion type that varies with content, with time of day, and with "mood." Some people hide certain emotions as a matter of course or express them obliquely, whereas others let them be evident, some employing deliberate purpose and skill lest the message be missed. The astute practical simulator would be alert to these dimensions of variability and make allowances when necessary.

If vicarious affective responses can be exploited for hypotheticoemotional reasoning, what need have we for a theory of emotions? To make *verbal attributions* of emotions, to ourselves as well as to others, might require a theory, at least an intuitive grasp of the causal structures described in the earlier chapters of this book. But verbal attribution would seem to play no essential role in practical simulation. As in the case of belief attributions, its chief employment would be communicative, to enable us to share our simulations with others.

But if there is no essential role in practical simulation for a theory of emotions, there may, nonetheless, be a useful role. It is instructive to contrast two ways in which an actor playing a part might try to bridge between his character's situation and behavior. If one is a "method" actor, that is, of the Stanislavsky–Strasberg school, one would typically do this by inducing in oneself an "as if" emotion that would fill the bill, leading one "naturally" to act as the script requires in the simulated situation specified by the script. One might strive for naturalness in execution by reviving remembered emotional reactions of one's own, but one would keep this real emotion subservient to the scripted inputs and outputs.

But inducing in oneself an emotion, even an "as if" emotion, would not be the only way to interpose between scripted situation and scripted behavior a causal structure corresponding to one of the emotions. Rather than become angry or even "as if" angry, the actor might simply recognize the situation, once he has put himself into it, as of a sort that might produce anger, and recognize the scripted behavior as of a sort that might be produced by such anger. He infers that the behavior is best accounted for by anger, and he knows how his character would comport himself in the situation if he were angry; yet he does all this without looping the inference, so to speak, through his own emotion-producing system. He uses a theory instead. This does not require that he be able to cite the relevant features of either the situation or the behavior, such as those qualifying it as one that might cause, or be caused by, anger. It is enough that he can recognize the situation intuitively as of a sort that satisfies the conceptual prerequisites of anger, and that he know intuitively what would, or could, constitute an angry response to that situation. Such "implicit knowledge" might even have some advantages over vicarious affect, for it is likely to be more constant and more readily accessible, less dependent on the availability of emotional memories of one's own and less likely to be biased by one's present mood.

This suggests that even if I am right in identifying folk psychology with practical simulation, there is a place for a common-sense theory of emotions. Although on a simulational account folk psychology is not itself a theory, in the accepted sense of (roughly) a system of laws implicitly defining a set of terms, it may provide a context within which open-ended generalizations, laws, and theories may be put to work. The job that might be performed by our personal repertoire of vicarious affective reactions might also

154

be performed – more reliably, in some respects – by a theoretical repertoire: a gallery of hypothetical pathways, so to speak, between situations of various types and behavior of various types, exemplifying causal structures other than straight practical reasoning. To explicate our implicit knowledge of these pathways is to set out the commonsense theory of emotions.

That is what I have attempted in this book. My first aim has been to provide a systematic framework within which can be mapped the full variety of causal structures we distinguish in our common talk. A second aim has been to answer some long-standing questions: among them, What distinguishes one emotion from another? What is it for an emotion to be *about* something? What differentiates emotions from *actions* and accounts for the intuition that we are not responsible for our emotions in quite the same way as for our actions?

For both these aims the distinction between *factive* and *epistemic* emotions has been pivotal. This is a lean, spare distinction, I grant; to focus on it is to neglect the variety and complexity of the particular factive and epistemic emotions we can distinguish in human beings. Yet the general distinction offers a framework within which finer discriminations and more complex explications can readily be made. And without such a framework – perhaps not exactly this one, but at least some powerful organizing structure – philosophical discussions of the emotions often degenerate to something comparable to "descriptions of the shapes of the rocks on a New Hampshire farm." Finally, one needs little more than the factive-epistemic distinction to demonstrate the poverty of a conceptual scheme of cognitive and attitudinal states – beliefs and desires, expectations and utilities, or subjective probabilities and preferences – that does without emotion concepts. To forgo these concepts, as I have argued, is to ignore common knowledge of the "chemistry" of cognitive and attitudinal states, the patterns and effects of their coaction in human beings.

155

References

Ager, T. A. 1984. "Computation in the Philosophy Curriculum." *Computers and the Humanities* 18:145–56.

Aristotle. *Rhetoric*, translated by W. D. Ross. New York: Oxford University Press, 1924.

Armstrong, D. M. 1968. *A Materialist Theory of the Mind*. London: Routledge & Kegan Paul.

Baron-Cohen, S., A. M. Leslie, and U. Frith. 1985. "Does the Autistic Child Have a 'Theory of Mind'?" *Cognition* 21:37–46.

Bedford, E. 1956–7. "Emotions." *Proceedings of the Aristotelian Society* 57:281–304.

Chisholm, R. M. 1957. *Perceiving: A Philosophical Study*. Ithaca, N.Y.: Cornell University Press.

Collingwood, R. G. 1946. *The Idea of History*, New York: Oxford University Press.

Davidson, D. 1963. "Actions, Reasons, and Causes." *Journal of Philosophy* 60:685–700. Reprinted in D. Davidson, *Essays on Actions and Events*. New York: Oxford University Press, 1980.

Davidson, D. 1968. "On Saying That." *Synthese* 17:130–46. Reprinted in D. Davidson, *Inquiries into Truth and Interpretation*. New York: Oxford University Press, 1984.

Davidson, D. 1976. "Hume's Cognitive Theory of Pride." *Journal of Philosophy* 73:744–56.

Davis, W. In press. "The Varieties of Fear." *Philosophical Studies*.

Doyle, A. Conan. 1894. "The Musgrave Ritual," in *The Memoirs of Sherlock Holmes*. New York: Harper Bros.

Dretske, F. 1971. "Conclusive Reasons." *Australasian Journal of Philosophy* 49:1–21.

Duffy, E. 1941. "An Explanation of 'Emotional' Phenomena Without the Use of the Concept 'Emotion.'" *Journal of General Psychology* 25:283–93.

Gettier, E. 1963. "Is Justified True Belief Knowledge?" *Analysis* 23:121–23.

Goldman, A. I. 1967. "A Causal Theory of Knowing." *Journal of Philosophy* 64:357–72.

Goldman, A. I. 1970. *A Theory of Human Action*. Englewood Cliffs, N.J.: Prentice-Hall.

Gordon, R. M. 1969. "Emotions and Knowledge." *Journal of Philosophy* 66:408–13.

156

Gordon, R. M. 1973. "Judgmental Emotions." *Analysis* 34:40–48.

Gordon, R. M. 1974. "The Aboutness of Emotions." *American Philosophical Quarterly* 11:27–36.

Gordon, R. M. 1978. "Emotion Labeling and Cognition." *Journal for the Theory of Social Behavior* 8:125–35.

Gordon, R. M. 1980. "Fear." *The Philosophical Review* 89:560–78.

Gordon, R. M. 1984. "A Causal Role for 'Conscious' Seeing." *The Behavioral and Brain Sciences* 7:628.

Gordon, R. M. 1986a. "Desire and Self-Intervention." *Noûs* 20:221–38.

Gordon, R. M. 1986b. "The Circle of Desire," in J. Marks, *The Ways of Desire*. Chicago: Precedent Publishing.

Gordon, R. M. 1986c. "The Passivity of Emotions." *The Philosophical Review* 95:339–60.

Grandy, R. 1973. "Reference, Meaning, and Belief." *Journal of Philosophy* 70:439–52.

Grice, H. P. 1957. "Meaning." *The Philosophical Review* 66:377–88.

Hebb, D. O. 1946. "Emotion in Man and Animal: An Analysis of the Intuitive Processes of Recognition." *Psychological Review* 53:88–106.

Heider, F. 1958. *The Psychology of Interpersonal Relations*. New York: Wiley.

James, W. 1884. "What Is an Emotion?" *Mind* 9 (O.S.):188–205.

James, W. 1890. *Principles of Psychology*. 2 vols. New York: Holt.

James, W. 1911. "The Physical Basis of Emotions." *Psychological Review* 1:516–609.

James, W., and C. G. Lange. 1885. *The Emotions*. Baltimore: William & Wilkins.

Kenny, A. 1963. *Action, Emotion, and Will*. London: Routledge & Kegan Paul.

Kiparsky, P., and C. Kiparsky. 1970. "Fact," in M. Bierwisch and K. E. Heidolph, *Progress in Linguistics: A Collection of Papers*. The Hague: Mouton.

Lazarus, R. S. 1966. *Psychological Stress and the Coping Process*. New York: McGraw-Hill.

Leslie, A. M. 1985. "Pretense and Representation in Infancy: The Origins of 'Theory of Mind.' " Unpublished manuscript.

Marañon, G. 1924. "Contribution à l'étude de l'action émotive de l'adrénaline." *Revue Française d'Endocrinologie* 21:301–25.

Morton, A. 1980. *Frames of Mind*. Oxford: Oxford University Press.

Nozick, R. 1981. *Philosophical Explanations*. Cambridge, Mass.: Harvard University Press.

Peters, R. S. 1961–2. "Emotions and the Category of Passivity." *Proceedings of the Aristotelian Society* 62:117–42.

Plutchik, R., and A. F. Ax. 1967. "A Critique of *Determinants of Emotional State* by Schachter and Singer." *Psychophysiology* 4:79–81.

Premack, D., and G. Woodruff. 1978. "Does the Chimpanzee Have a Theory of Mind?" *The Behavioral and Brain Sciences* 1:515–26.

Putnam, H. 1978. *Meaning and the Moral Sciences*. London: Routledge & Kegan Paul.

Quine, W. V. O. 1960. *Word and Object*. Cambridge, Mass.: MIT Press.

157

Russell, B. 1960. *An Outline of Philosophy*. Cleveland: World.

Sankowski, E. 1977. "Responsibility of Persons for Their Emotions." *Canadian Journal of Philosophy* 7:829–40.

Schachter, S. 1959. *The Psychology of Affiliation: Experimental Studies of the Sources of Gregariousness*. Stanford, Calif.: Stanford University Press.

Schachter, S. 1971. *Emotion, Obesity, and Crime*. New York: Academic Press.

Schachter, S., and J. E. Singer. 1962. "Cognitive, Social, and Physiological Determinants of Emotional State." *Psychological Review* 69:379–99.

Schutz, A. 1962. *Collected Papers*. The Hague: Nijhoff.

Schutz, A. 1967. *Phenomenology and the Social World*. Evanston, Ill.: Northwestern University Press.

Searle, J. R. 1983. *Intentionality: An Essay in the Philosophy of Mind*. Cambridge: Cambridge University Press.

Skyrms, B. 1967. "The Explication of X Knows that *p*," *Journal of Philosophy* 64:373–89.

Solomon, R. C. 1973. "Emotions and Choice." *The Review of Metaphysics* 27:20–41.

Solomon, R. C. 1977. *The Passions*. New York: Doubleday.

Spinoza, B. *Ethics*, translated by R. H. M. Elwes. London: George Bell & Sons, 1883.

Stich, S. 1983. *From Folk Psychology to Cognitive Science: The Case Against Belief*. Cambridge, Mass.: MIT Press.

Thalberg, I. 1964. "Emotion and Thought." *American Philosophical Quarterly* 1:45–55.

Unger, P. 1967. "Experience and Factual Knowledge." *Journal of Philosophy* 64:152–73.

Unger, P. 1975. *Ignorance*. New York: Oxford University Press.

Wilson, J. R. S. 1972. *Emotion and Object*. Cambridge: Cambridge University Press.

Wimmer, H., and J. Perner. 1983. "Beliefs About Beliefs: Representation and Constraining Function of Wrong Beliefs in Young Children's Understanding of Deception." *Cognition* 13:103–28.

Wittgenstein, L. 1953. *Philosophical Investigations*. New York: Macmillan.

Wright, G. H. von 1971. *Explanation and Understanding*. Ithaca, N.Y.: Cornell University Press.

158

Index

159